THE CRISIS GAME

SIMULATING INTERNATIONAL CONFLICT

THE CRISIS GAME
SIMULATING INTERNATIONAL CONFLICT

SIDNEY F. GIFFIN

Doubleday & Company, Inc., Garden City, New York, 1965

PREFACE

Followers of the Steve Canyon strip will remember that
Copper Calhoon was shown, a year or two back, participating in a Pentagon "cold war" game. She was found in the
denouement enjoying the embraces of an—ugh!—labor
leader, a fellow gamer who somehow discerned the charm
beneath her veneer of venom. It seems apparent that a gaming device which could move Milton Caniff's disagreeable
lady magnate into so unfamiliar a posture deserves close
attention. My reason for devoting attention to gaming,
however, has little to do with the Steve Canyon episode
(regrettably, because any author hates to abandon romantic
interest on his first page). The fact is that an explanation
and evaluation of free, crisis gaming deserves doing and
has not been done. A modest literature has grown up on
the subject in the past ten years, largely in article form
and in considerable part unpublished. Nowhere to my
knowledge is there publicly available any considerable, ap-
propriately illustrated description of crisis-game technique,
nor any effort to place this kind of exercise in the context of
conflict gaming as a whole. While the attention devoted
to related activities will be introductory at best, I will attempt to make a technique of crisis gaming wholly evident.

If crisis gaming can be considered useful in Washington
governmental circles, as a recent spate of such gaming
serves to suggest, it may also prove useful elsewhere and in

academic circles. In a few universities it has already been employed. The number may grow if the technique is widely available, assuming of course that it can be regarded as having academic utility. I think it does have academic utility, as I hope the chapters to follow will demonstrate, although I am also willing to admit, and even to proclaim, sharp limitations on this utility.

A survey of the subject which is serious without being portentous—and, I should now say, the primary subject is the plausible simulation of possible situations involving international conflict, resolution of which ought to be accomplished without either a compromise of vital interests or a resort to major warfare—may even prove useful in Washington. A forceful figure will surely appear one day in the Pentagon or elsewhere in government, possessed of no gaming experience but convinced that any such activity is another folly of the preceding (Republican) (Democratic) Administration. This will end Washington gaming for that time. In fact, a pause could come for other reasons, such as too many real crises over too long a period. In any event, the live art could easily disappear from the Washington scene.

Suppose in this circumstance an extended period of international calm were to develop? In due course, responsible officials would then come to lose that feel for crisis management which they have had ample opportunity to acquire during recent decades of international static. The simulation of crisis management could then become an indispensable adjunct to federal office at the policy and decision levels, and at the levels advisory to policy makers, because surely there has never been a time when the management and control of crises required better understanding. The high political staffs of superpowers ought to be

8

drawn from among those who have trained and prepared for crisis management, as senior military officers have long trained and prepared for the conduct of war. When crises do not exist, therefore, they ought occasionally to be invented. In any event, it should not be necessary, in a revival of Washington crisis gaming, to start afresh without benefit of a textbook—and those who think recourse could be had to the files can have had no experience either of the files or of Washington.

My hope, therefore, is that I will offer sufficient information on crisis gaming, together with sufficient example, so that readers of professional competence may themselves attempt this absorbing activity upon some basis of experience. At the least, they should be better able to judge the claims and results emerging from the crisis games of others.

More than most books, this one owes its main debt to a narrow circle of specialists who are also innovators. They are James Adams of the Stanford Research Institute (formerly director of cold war gaming for the Joint Chiefs of Staff), Lincoln P. Bloomfield of the Massachusetts Institute of Technology, and Thomas C. Schelling of Harvard. I have had the opportunity to work with each of these three in crisis games for which they bore, respectively, the chief responsibility. If there exist any practitioners of crisis gaming more accomplished, I for one do not know them, and many of the ideas in this book have been acquired from one or the other or all three.

I will cover several current activities related to crisis gaming in Chapter III, and it should be acknowledged that this chapter will expose most of what I know about those activities. The flow diagram appearing there does so through the kindness of a mathematical colleague, John Wells. The content of Chapter VII will be found to derive from a crisis game conducted at the Institute for Defense Analyses, with the help of other colleagues whose courtesy I want to acknowledge. They are Alvin Cottrell, David Crist, James Cross, Robert Gessert, Laszlo Hadik, Walter Hahn, Harold Hinton, Nehemiah Jordan, James King, Adele Scaraton, John Tashjean, Stanislaw Wasowski, and Donald Weller. I owe an added heavy debt to Cross, Jordan, Tashjean, and Miss Scaraton for their helpful reading of my manuscript. I want to thank Peggy Duggin, Shirley Phillips, and those other young ladies who, with skill and patience, fed my revisions through their typewriters.

The Institute for Defense Analyses deserves my special gratitude for affording me the opportunity to put this little book together. It obviously bears no responsibility for the opinions expressed.

Shortcomings in the work are of course entirely my own.

Sidney F. Giffin   March 1965
Institute for Defense Analyses
Arlington, Virginia

CONTENTS

Chapter I
THE WAR GAME GENESIS[1]

Crisis gaming is in one current of a notable gaming history that goes back to chess, and therefore of course to such progenitors of that ancient pastime as draughts or checkers. The Russians, whose regard for chess equals that of others for football, cricket, or the late, late show, have nevertheless modestly neglected to claim its invention. Their restraint seems well justified, because chess appeared in an approximation of its present form a millennium before the Swedes, by organizing Muscovy, in effect invented Russia.

Most authorities are agreed that chess originated in India. It had the Sanskrit name *chaturanga,* which describes an army composed of elephants, horses, chariots, and infantry. Pieces used in the original Hindu game represented the same four elements of an army, and the supporting frame of the

[1] I am indebted throughout this chapter and the next to E. A. Raymond and Harry W. Baer, Jr., "A History of War Games," *The Reserve Officer,* Vol. XV, No. 10, October 1938, pp. 19–20; to John P. Young, *A Survey of Historical Developments in War Games,* ORO Report SP-98, March 1959; and to William Cowper, *The Game of War,* Technical Operations, Inc., Burlington, Mass., 1960. Source of the historical basis of chess is the Encyclopaedia Britannica, 1959 edition. Young's article provides an excellent bibliography of source material. Another fine bibliography is contained in Francis J. McHugh, *Fundamentals of War Gaming,* the Naval War College, 1961.

chessboard employed today presumably symbolizes the wall of a fortified city.

From India, chess made its way to Persia in the seventh century A.D. Persian writers on the subject are frank to admit the debt to India, thereby dealing a blow to claims that the game was invented by, among others, themselves, the Greeks, Romans, Babylonians, Chinese, or Arabians. During its passage of Persia, *chaturanga* changed its name to *shatranj,* and the present "checkmate" apparently derives from *shah mat,* "the king is dead."

The manner in which the various pieces have been permitted to move has changed sharply over the centuries. *Shatranj* evolved into modern chess during the fifteenth century in France, and then moved to Spain in order to produce the first distinguished writer on the subject, Ruy Lopez de Sigura.

As a war game, its practitioners must admit that chess leaves much to be desired. If, as Jomini said, strategy is the "art of making war on a map," the checkered board of chess provides only a sharply stylized field for combat. The rules are rigid and, in terms of warfare, artificial to an extreme. However, a semblance of realism does obtain. The king is about as restricted in his movements as a pawn. The maximum latitude accorded any of the pieces goes to the only woman in the game. And the moves of the bishops are slanted—properly so, in occasional cases, if we may learn anything from the behavior of President Makarios of Cyprus.

The spirit of chess, however intellectualized, undoubtedly approaches that of war, and it is not surprising to find military men at the beginning of modern history supporting chess as a form of mental and moral discipline. It is also not surprising that they began to find it increasingly less adequate in this respect, for warfare was beginning to exhibit a formalism of its own that had little resemblance to the formalism of chess. Thus there commenced efforts to devise more and more realistic war games with which military students might be trained or amused or, preferably, both.

It must be recalled that military officers, unlike other professional men, lack the opportunity to practice their trade except under the special circumstances of war. And, even then, one war can differ so much from another that for many practical purposes past experience can be more hindrance than help in approaching what comes next. Once war is joined, it provides its own classroom. Military men then acquire competence of the kind that seems to be required for the occasion.[2] However, this can be a terribly costly way to learn during initial stages of ignorance, and the search for *ersatz* experience in anticipation of battle never ends. Especially during periods of technological change, when new and untried weapons enter the armed forces, the adaptation by military forces to their capabilities and limitations demands imagination, experimentation, maneuvers, and games.

Historically, war games have never represented a means of arriving at those new concepts of organization and tactics that are always essential for the assimilation of new weapons to best effect. They have provided, rather, a useful means of inculcating concepts already formed, of emphasizing rules and planning factors, and of affording practice in the field of decision-making.

The highest objective of the war game has generally been

[2] One can suspect that this truism will not apply to an extensive exchange of nuclear weapons. Where violence is kept within manageable limits, the rules will presumably continue to apply.

to train future military commanders to arrive at sound decisions despite inadequate knowledge of the enemy and despite inevitable, and hence normal, errors and miscarriages on the part of friendly forces. Games of this type can of course best be conducted as field maneuvers using live men and real equipment, if not, as czarist troops are reported to have used, live ammunition. Maneuvers are manifestly expensive and, at some times of the year in some locales, are likely to prove impracticable. For convenience, substitutes for war and even field exercises have accordingly long been devised on the basis of cards, maps, or sand tables. Nowadays, using maps having transparent overlays, forces can be readily maneuvered with grease pencils. The practice in the past, by no means wholly abandoned, was to move pins or blocks, the latter often made to scale and representing bodies of troops, ships, etc. March tables, firing tables, and similar "canned" aids are employed to assist in defining combat possibilities, although an umpire or umpires may also decide the issue on the basis of judgment. Where probabilities are involved, which is not infrequent, cards have been drawn or dice thrown.

Until after Napoleon, even complicated war games amounted to no more than ingenious adaptations of chess. The first of these appeared in 1644, the invention of Christopher Weikhmann of Prussia, and was called the "King's Game" or "military chess." It involved fourteen varieties of moves for thirty pieces on each side: a king, officers, chancellors, heralds, couriers, chaplains, adjutants, bodyguards, halberdiers, and private soldiers (the pawns). This game attempted to incorporate some of the military ideas of the period, and hence provided, better than regular chess, a vehicle for the cadet's study of war and maneuver. The names of some of the pieces in this game suggest that it allowed for political as well as military maneuvering.

The next development in the field occurred in France during the early eighteenth century. This time cards were utilized to develop two games, the first being called *le jeu de la guerre*. At a time when sieges provided most of the significant operations in warfare, it was probably inevitable that a companion game should be devised, *le jeu de la fortification,* stressing siege principles. The military symbols carried on the cards were in fact designed to impress upon students the going military facts and principles.

In the latter half of the eighteenth century, especially in Prussia, there occurred what was later known as the "vogue of military mathematics." Warfare came to be regarded as an exact science having largely geometrical applications. Cadets of the Berlin Military Academy were absorbed in Kant's philosophical reliance on mathematics as well as in his 1795 proposal, "Perpetual Peace," based upon a federation of free states. Ability to calculate was considered essential in military leaders. (The informed reader may detect similarities between this period in Prussia and that of today in the United States. Certainly the United States needs military Ph.D.'s capable of coping with the gadgetry supplied by civilian Ph.D.'s. Also, our military people often exhibit a certain nervous interest in successive proposals touching the question of disarmament.) War games of the time followed the fashion by relying heavily on mathematics in design and play. But at the height of the mathematical vogue, in Brunswick, there was developed one of the last and most complicated innovations among games stemming directly from chess. This was called Helwig's game, from the master of pages at the Brunswick court.

Helwig's game used a modified chessboard which carried

1666 movable squares variously colored to represent terrain features. Thus, black and white indicated level ground; red, inaccessible mountains; green, impassable swamps; and blue, lakes or rivers. A string of blue squares defined a river demanding passage by pontoons. Numbers on the squares were employed to indicate special terrain features. Dividing the board was a dotted line that marked the frontier between the opposing camps, and each theater of operations was composed of a number of provinces identified by letters. The object of the game was to capture the opponent's fortification, in one corner of his side and marked about with symbols to suggest such defenses as ditches and parapets.

Sizable forces were assigned to each side; for example, sixty battalions of fusiliers, or infantry, doubling on occasion as artillery, eight squadrons of dragoons, or cavalry, and 100 pontoon boats. The game progressed under a director who enforced the application of strict rules defining the movement and employment of infantry, artillery, cavalry, and the remaining specialized pieces. Again, there resulted an exceedingly formal game, the rigidities of which were relieved only by the feature that the combat terrain could be broadly redesigned for each succeeding play of the board.

Helwig's game was followed in short order by another of the same type, developed in Schleswig and called *neue Kriegsspiel*. (Kriegsspiel translates literally as "war game.") This one had 3600 squares and was accompanied by a sixty-page book of rules. The complexity of the game was exceeded only by its tedium, which may be one reason why the development of the war game took a subsequent sharp twist.

But this twist certainly also resulted from Napoleonic

practice, which, by utilizing massed national armies and rapid maneuver, brought about great changes in the art and character of warfare. The resulting complications could hardly be represented with anything approaching reality on the basis of even the most ingenious modification of chess. As usual, it was in Prussia—this time at Breslau—that a new game appeared. The notion of M. von Reisswitz, it moved war gaming from a modified chessboard to a sand table. This permitted the reproduction of terrain features in miniature. It was an honest attempt to develop something that might have real and practical military utility, and it led directly to the emergence of one significant type of war game that has remained basically the same ever since.

This game was developed by von Reisswitz, Jr., as a member of the Prussian Guard Artillery, in 1824. His contribution was to transfer gaming to maps and thus to adapt war gaming to the simulation of actual military operations. (It might be noted that Napoleon himself was apparently the initial tactician to use colored pins on detailed maps for the purpose of planning his campaigns in advance.) The first distinguished patron of von Reisswitz, Jr., Prince William I, who later became emperor of Germany, brought the game to the attention of King Frederick William III and Marshal von Meffling. The latter, after his first review of von Reisswitz, Jr.'s work, exclaimed with real excitement, "It is not a game at all! It's a training for war! I shall recommend it most emphatically to the whole army." Helped by other officers and urged on by his patrons, von Reisswitz, Jr., produced a set of rules and directions called *Instructions for the Representation of Tactical Maneuvers under the Guise of a War Game.* Supplements followed in 1825 and again in 1828, and von Reisswitz, Jr., was called upon to supervise the preparation of new and improved maps.

Because this game gradually achieved acceptance in the armies of many nations and remains the prototype of much modern war gaming, it repays examination in some detail.

The maps used represented about four square miles of ground on a scale of one to 8000. The details of terrain were as full as the art of topography then permitted and, while not drawn from actual terrain, were highly realistic. Leaden blocks representing the troops employed were made to scale. They were colored to indicate opposing sides, a practice that obtains today in U.S. games, where our side is always true blue and the baddies carry a red stigma. Conventional signs were marked on the blocks to define the type and number of troops portrayed, whether a battalion of infantry, a squadron of cavalry, or a battery of artillery. Other paraphernalia included scales of ranges and distances, dividers and dice.

Each side had a commander, who might have a limited number of subordinates. But the *deus ex machina* was the umpire, whose decisions were above question and who demanded that all maneuvers stay within the drill regulations. The umpire signaled the start of each game by providing both commanders with a "general hypothesis" describing the over-all situation and gave each a "special theme" outlining his own position of attack or defense, this latter being designed to promote a rapid contact of the belligerent forces.

The umpire required that all orders, reports, and plans be furnished to him, so that he might be in a position to forestall fantastic situations, feed intelligence to each side at appropriate times, and judge generally the execution of play. Every action passed through the umpire and the opposing players had to remain silent. Time was the controlling factor of the game, being divided into two-minute intervals, called rounds. No movement or action could occur within a round unless it was considered, in terms of planning factors or regulations as interpreted by the all-powerful umpire, to be reasonable and practicable within this period. It was common practice to stop the game after each round in order to assess losses and to examine the resulting situation in detail.

Players obviously had to be familiar with the functions and tactics of each combat arm, while the umpire had to be an officer of recognized ability and experience. From the initial conditions, often devised by himself, and the initial written orders issued by each commander, the umpire developed the starting situation. Troop elements not masked from enemy sight by terrain features were then placed on the map, and additional elements appeared on the map as they in turn became subject to enemy visual reconnaissance. Time was carefully calculated, so that lapses were required, for example, to permit the transmission of information from patrols or for the passage of orders to combat units. In a day when electronics was yet to become an essential, if complicated, adjunct to military operations, it was reasonable to suppose that orders could not be effectively transmitted beyond a distance of some 1000 meters, and this again was a condition of the game.

When units came under fire or encountered obstacles, losses and other mischances were determined by a throw of as many as seven dice from combinations of which judgments had been predetermined. An inferior force might thus impel the foe to withdraw with heavy casualties if the luck of the dice was exceptionally good.

The efforts of the younger von Reisswitz had a melancholy sequel. The favor in which he was held by Prince William and others of exalted rank brought upon him an envy within the army which resulted in his transfer to exceptionally dull garrison duty at the border post of Torgau. He took his own life there in 1827, disillusioned at the failure of his patrons to protect his interests.

Despite the royal interest displayed in von Reisswitz's game, it did not achieve extensive use even in the Prussian Army for almost two decades. It survived because clubs of officers formed here and there in garrison towns to experiment with its possibilities, and because journals and game proceedings were maintained to provide for an exchange of information among club members. Through translation of these papers, the game spread in one form or another, as the century wore on, to England, France, Austria-Hungary, Russia, Italy, Turkey, Japan, and the United States. Foreign interest in the Prussian-developed war game became marked only after the successes enjoyed by Prussian arms in 1866 over Austria-Hungary. War gaming was thereafter made obligatory in the Austrian Army. The following quotation[3] suggests a possible reason:

> . . . In general, in an [Austrian] army that revered the name of Radetzky, gallantry and dash were more widely respected than the methodical but inconspicuous work that turns an armed force into a well-functioning machine. . . . it is not surprising that staff work was not highly regarded in the Austrian Army, and that the staff system was ineffective. In 1854, the Prussian military attaché in Vienna had found it impossible to interest his Austrian colleagues in the *Kriegsspiel* used to train Prussian staff officers once he admitted that it was not a game at which one could win money; and Lieutenant Colonel (later *Feldzeugmeister*)

[3] Craig, Gordon A., *The Battle of Königgrätz*, J. B. Lippincott Company, Philadelphia & New York, 1964, pp. 10–11.

Friedrich Freiherr von Beck, who was serving on the staff of the Vienna Army Command at about the same time, admitted that among his fellows there were only one or two officers with even a rudimentary understanding of their jobs. Ten years later, when Beck was a member of the Geographical Bureau of the General Staff, he was charged with the job of making a military-geographical study of central Germany. He was supposed to base his report on surveys and maps sent to him by one of his superiors, who had gone to Germany to prepare them. This officer, however, preferred to spend his time in the casinos at Bad Ems and answered Beck's pleas for material by writing that he could find everything that he needed in Baedeker!

In the United States, until 1879, there appeared several versions of war games, most of them of limited interest because they were either based on chess or on the von Reisswitz game. At this time Major W. R. Livermore, U.S. Army Corps of Engineers, produced a significant American contribution to war gaming.[4] Using Prussian developments as his base, Livermore introduced to the war game Civil War experience and that of other wars since Napoleon. Idealized geography was again employed, together with conventional topographic signs and small blocks to represent troop elements. However, each side now possessed its own map in a room separated from that of the "enemy." The umpires were thus in a position to provide to the opposing commanders less than the full information concerning the enemy that was always available when both forces were deployed on a single map. This device at once introduced an element of realism going well beyond any previously attained, for it became possible to develop a game atmosphere approach-

[4] *The American Kriegsspiel*, Houghton Mifflin Company, Boston, 1882.

23

ing the actual "fog of war." Livermore also employed numerous new or improved devices to sharpen and speed up play. Included were numerous charts and tables developed to cover in practical detail most of the events that might occur in maneuver or battle; for example, variations in the march rate of infantry over different types of terrain and for varying rates of climb or descent. His tables on occasion show a startling relationship to the mathematical models now prepared for computer solution. (See Chapter III.)

Although the Livermore game remained captive to its numerous rules, the claim could be made that virtually any aspect of warfare could be represented on its map. Certainly, a tactical engagement could be played in detail, and a complete battle could be represented in general. Strategy, involving the maneuvers of armies over time and extensive areas, could be displayed. In addition, both naval warfare and coastal operations were possible.

Nine years after the first naval game was developed by Captain Philip H. Colomb of the British Navy, the notion of gaming was introduced to the U.S. Naval War College in a series of lectures by William McCarty Little. A retired naval lieutenant, Little served for twenty-eight years thereafter as gaming consultant on the staff of the college until his death in 1915. His unofficial title as the first professional American war gamer appears unchallengeable.

The naval gaming that thus began under Little's tutelage, at a time when Captain Alfred Thayer Mahan was President of the Naval War College, has continued to the present day. There have been changes. The original games involved a duel between two battleships and a "fleet" game representing the interactions between two hostile squadrons of battleships and cruisers. A "strategic" game then evolved, in

24

which plans of fleet maneuver were required to bring about contact with an opposing fleet.

The full scope of war had been played at Newport before World War II. Fleet Admiral Chester W. Nimitz was able to say, in lecturing before the college during October 1960: "The war with Japan had been re-enacted in the game rooms here by so many people and in so many different ways that nothing that happened during the war was a surprise—absolutely nothing except the Kamikaze tactics toward the end of the war. . . ."[5] (The incident at Pearl Harbor must have been excluded from "during the war.")

In our own century there has of course developed an entertaining offshoot of the serious war game, the miniature war involving carefully molded and painted lead soldiers together with realistic model fortifications, guns, tanks, and other paraphernalia that contribute to an illusion of reality. This kind of play can become very elaborate, a hobby along the lines of model railroading. In *How to Play War Games in Miniature,*[6] Joseph Morschauer III provides most of the information needed for the potential hobbyist. He points out that one can select an historical period of special interest, such as the period of the American Revolution or of the Napoleonic Wars, and obtain the types of figures appropriate to the time. In addition to basic rules for play, he suggests the rules applicable to each period of warfare, rules tailored to the weapons and tactics then in vogue. These rules again are quite rigid, leading generally to a decisive throw of dice. If you have kept your Confederate money, here is one way to reverse the decision of 1865!

[5] *U. S. Naval Institute Proceedings,* March 1964, p. 52.
[6] Walker & Co., New York, 1962.

Chapter II
EMERGENCE OF THE FREE GAME

Free Kriegsspiel, as it will shortly be described, did not emerge as a practical tool for soldiers until more than a century after it made an initial isolated appearance in France. Guibert, whose *Essay général de tactique* of 1770 would impress Bonaparte with the importance of mobility, was early inspired to an interest in warfare by his father, the Comte de Guibert, about whose training he had this to say:

My mind was scarce opened when he gave me the first lessons of the tactic. He successively taught me by words, by diagrams, and on the ground; when I had once acquired a just conception of its elements, he dissected on pasteboard a variety of movable figured plans, with which all kinds of ground could be represented. On these plans he demonstrated to me, with small wooden blocks, all the mechanism of armies. He showed me a representation of battles which could furnish apt examples; he more particularly showed me those of the war that was then in progress, and of which the details and events had the most attracted my attention; subsequently I had to apply my *coup d'œil* and judgment on all kinds of ground. On returning home we would resume our game. He allowed me to make objections. He allowed me to exercise my own imagination. Insensibly it acquired more extension and justness. We next formed two armies and each took command of one of them. Then in different types of country, represented at chance by the arrangement of the pasteboard plans, we made our armies manœuvre; we made them execute marches; we made choice of positions; we formed in order of battle one against the other. We afterwards reasoned out between ourselves what we had done. My father encouraged my questions, and even contrary opinions. The nights frequently passed in this occupation, so much did this study absorb us, so well did my teacher know how to make it interesting.[1]

But it was not until after the Austro-Prussian and Franco-German wars of 1866 and 1870 that it became the habit for military officers, beginning (as we might expect) in Germany, to undertake tactical rides or staff maneuvers. While covering actual ground, although with imaginary troops, maneuvers were simulated, artillery fire laid on, and attack and defense developed from carefully written orders and messages. These documents, marked for time and place, then formed the basis for decisions by an umpire. No rules were prescribed to govern events, the umpires relying instead wholly upon their own judgment and experience.

To at least one instructor in the German Army, Colonel von Verdy du Vernois, it seemed evident that the same freedom of conduct that characterized the tactical ride should obtain for the play of war on a map. His call for this type of gaming in 1876 divided the practice of war gaming into rigid Kriegsspiel, emphasizing control by rules, and free Kriegsspiel, emphasizing control by an umpire, each of which has its proponents to the present day.

[1] This quotation is derived from *The Ghost of Napoleon*, by B. H. Liddell Hart, Yale University Press, New Haven, 1934. His bibliography indicates that Guibert's essay was translated into English in 1781.

The new free game, uncomplicated as it was by rules, placed a heavy burden on the umpire or director. But his decisions could be questioned following each exercise, as the decisions of dice and a rule book could not, and while military propriety and discipline kept the questioning within bounds, it now became possible to conduct illuminating critiques after each play of a free game. The principal intitial purpose, although others developed later, was to provide extremely vivid peacetime training for young officers in the conduct of field operations. Specific actions could be undertaken in maneuvering forces toward conflict, and to a lesser extent, *in* conflict, about which there could be differences of opinion but upon which at least enlightenment and possibly even a consensus could finally be reached. All participants, including the umpires, were likely to learn something from such an exercise.

The game was again based upon accurate maps, although now divided between small-scale maps, covering large areas for purposes of strategic maneuver, and large-scale maps for the conduct of battle. Blocks again represented tactical units, if without much concern as to scale. Two opposed groups of players were formed under the direction of the umpire. At an umpire briefing, the players learned the general situation to be faced, and then each side was apprised of its own peculiar situation. Each side then prepared for the umpire a set of orders and dispositions in order to start the play. For purposes of concealment, two rooms were used. Obviously, preparations for the game, initial situations, the maps with dividers, and the practice of separating the opposing sides derived from rigid Kriegsspiel in its later stages.

Umpiring was accomplished in a room containing the strategic small-scale map for the exercise, while the teams alternated in the use of a second room housing the detailed, large-scale map. In this second room one team worked out its latest moves as the other team, using the general map, informed the umpire of the moves it had similarly just accomplished. Marks made by one side on the detailed map were removed before the other side used the map. The umpire displayed only that information on the large-scale map as, in his opinion, would probably be available to both sides and hence should be seen by both.

Despite the lack of rules and tables, there was an evident need to have agreement on matters of military fact, such as the length of the column for each of a number of units or the rates of march of infantry and cavalry under varying conditions. These were generally known and accepted by players and umpires alike. Tactical maneuver was given the principal stress in free Kriegsspiel, to include decisions and orders required for the purpose of accomplishing contact with the enemy on favorable terms.

Although von Verdy's book on free Kriegsspiel was not published in the United States until 1897 in a translation by Major Eben Swift of the 5th U.S. Cavalry, enough was known of the content of this work to produce at least one protest that remains today the most valid of complaints about free war gaming. Major C. W. Raymond, Corps of Engineers, in a book called *Kriegsspiel,* published in 1881, had this to say:

> However possible such an exercise may be in Germany, it will certainly be found generally impracticable in our own country. In Berlin, where there are officers of the general staff who devote their undivided attention to the study of the art of war, it may be possible to obtain competent directors . . . but in this country . . . only in a few exceptional cases would it be possible to obtain a director, the

superiority of whose experience and attainments would be so undoubted that his decisions would receive unhesitating acceptance. [Raymond then went on to point out that the umpires, as they undergo the experience of umpiring, unconsciously or even consciously develop rules to assist the process of decision] . . . the choice we have to make is not between rules and no rules, but between rules based on the careful study of all available data . . . and rules extemporized by a single authority. . . .

If the decisions of a single authority had to be accepted without question, as Raymond suggested, the free game would indeed be subject to caprice. What was learned in one game might well have to be unlearned in the next. But question and discussion following the play are essential features of the free war game and of its outdoor companions, the training trip and the tactical walk, as all have developed to our own day. There should be, in such activities, no "school solution" to substitute for thinking on the part of the students or instructors, and even the distinction between students and instructors must be blurred. Something good is then likely to result, if no more than Clausewitz suggests when he says:[2]

> No general can give his army habituation to war, and maneuvers (peace exercises) furnish but a weak substitute for it, weak in comparison with real experience in war, but not weak in relation to other armies in which even these maneuvers are limited to mere mechanical exercises of routine. So to arrange the maneuvers in peacetime as to include . . . causes of friction . . . is of much greater value than those believe who do not know the thing from experience. It is of immense importance that the soldier, high or low, whatever his rank, should not see for the first time in

[2] *On War,* Infantry Journal Press, Washington, D.C., 1950.

30

war those phenomena of war which, when seen for the first time, astonish and perplex him. If he has only met them once before, even by that he is half acquainted with them.

While maneuvers therefore are undeniably useful, we need not become lyrical about them. The following excerpt from Evelyn Waugh[3] deals with a British battalion field maneuver in the early days of World War II. If the initials are incomprehensible, they do impart an authentic military flavor to the passage.

Presently the C.O. arrived. "Is this C Company?" he asked.

"Yes, sir."

"Well, what's happening? You ought to be on the start line by now." Then since it was clearly no use attacking Captain Brown about that, he said in a way Captain Brown had learned to dread: "I must have missed your sentries coming along. Just put me in the picture, will you, of your local defense?"

"Well, sir, we've just halted here. . . ."

The C.O. led Captain Brown away.

"He's getting a rocket[4]," said the anti-tank man. It was the first moment of satisfaction he had known that day.

Captain Brown came back looking shaken and began posting air look-outs and gas sentries with feverish activity. While he was in the middle of it the platoon orderlies came back to lead the platoons to assembly positions. Alastair advanced with the platoon another half mile. Then they halted. Mr. Smallwood appeared and collected the section-commanders around him. The C.O. was there too, listening to Mr. Smallwood's orders. When they were finished he

[3] *Put Out More Flags*, Little, Brown and Company, Boston, 1942, pp. 165–67.
[4] A bawling-out.

said, "I don't think you mentioned the R.A.P., did you, Smallwood?"

"R.A.P. sir? No, sir, I'm afraid I don't know where it is."

The C.O. led Mr. Smallwood out of hearing of his platoon.

"Now *he's* getting a rocket," said the anti-tank man with glee.

The section-commanders came back to their men. Mr. Smallwood's orders had been full of detail; start line, zero hour, boundaries inclusive and exclusive, objectives, supporting fire. "It's like this," said Corporal Deacon. "They're over there and we're here. So then we go for un."

Another half-hour passed. Captain Mayfield appeared. "For Christ's sake, Smallwood, you ought to be halfway up the ridge by this time."

"Oh," said Mr. Smallwood. "Sorry. Come on. Forward."

The platoon collected its equipment and toiled into action up the opposing slope. Major Bush, the second-in-command, appeared before them. They fired their blanks at him with enthusiasm. "Got him," said the man next to Alastair.

"You're coming under heavy fire," said the Major. "Most of you are casualties."

"He's a casualty himself."

"Well, what are you going to do, Smallwood?"

"Get down, sir."

"Well *get* down."

"Get down," ordered Mr. Smallwood.

"What are you going to do now?"

Mr. Smallwood looked round desperately for inspiration. "Put down smoke, sir."

"Well, *put* down smoke."

"Put down smoke," said Mr. Smallwood to Alastair.

The Major went on his way to confuse the platoon on their flank.

32

"Come on," said Mr. Smallwood. "We've got to get up this infernal hill sometime. We might as well do it now."

It was shorter than it looked; they were up in twenty minutes and at the summit there was a prolonged shambles. Bit by bit the whole battalion appeared from different quarters. C Company was collected and fallen in; then they were fallen out to eat their dinners. No one had any dinner left, so they lay on their backs and smoked.

The restrained words of praise which Clausewitz was able to give to the field maneuver quite patently apply also to free Kriegsspiel, as another reasonably faithful means of imitating war. Certainly in Germany the military interest in war gaming increased enormously with the introduction of free Kriegsspiel. But the normal dialectical process also produced a heightened interest in rigid Kriegsspiel. Uncompromising positions of opposition, as we have pointed out, were rapidly taken by advocates of one form or the other. In the closing years of the century, however, it began to be clear to most practitioners of war gaming that free and rigid Kriegsspiel were not in fact wholly divorced from each other, and that practical gaming might often draw something from each. In his book, *Kriegsspiel,* Major Raymond further commented:

> We find the writers on free Kriegsspiel occasionally admitting that rules and tables may sometimes be useful, and on the other hand, advocates of rigid Kriegsspiel generally begin with the statement that the rules and tables are intended to be merely of an advisory character and that the director should proceed without them whenever his personal knowledge suffices for the occasion. The distinction between the two systems is, indeed, largely one of degree; yet it is sufficiently marked to justify its recognition.

We shall see that crisis gaming derives from free Kriegsspiel and that rigid Kriegsspiel is a true predecessor of computer gaming. We shall also see that current combinations of man and machine for game purposes can be regarded as paralleling the compromise between free and rigid Kriegsspiel.

Free war gaming met with several innovations during the early decades of the twentieth century. First and most obvious was the introduction of maps drawn from actual rather than idealized ground. Battles considered significant to the continuing art of warfare could be refought, often with variations for purposes of study and experimentation, using the forces and terrain employed in the original. Transparent overlays of celluloid or glass were also used—an American innovation. Not only was this a more convenient means of demonstrating maneuvers, in that colored pencils could be employed more flexibly than could solid blocks, but it now became possible to retain a graphic record of play by employing a series of transparencies, a notion that sprang from work at the Naval War College at Newport. Also from the Naval War College came the useful practice of orienting overlays, with respect to maps or charts, so that the transparencies of both antagonists could be placed on the umpire's map, one on top of the other, in order to present him with an accurate, periodic overview of the developing situation.

In the United States, the first actual terrain map designed for game purposes was drawn, from surveys by students of the Army Staff College, to cover a tract near Fort Leavenworth, Kansas. The scale was one foot to the mile and the area shown was about four miles by six. But the terrain maps that no ripely mature graduate of the United States Military Academy can possibly forget are those of the area around Gettysburg. These were very detailed maps, again one foot to the mile and with twelve-foot contour intervals. They introduced the cadet to map maneuvers by immersing him in the famous Civil War battle. To this day, I occasionally find myself emerging from sleep with a muffled scream, a fugitive from the Little Round Top of a West Point map exercise. Others have also experienced military-map nightmares. As Field Marshal Sir William Slim suggests:[5]

"It has been decided, therefore," said the brigadier, "to take punitive action against Panch Pir."

"Yes, but where *is* the damn place," growled my colonel.

"I will now read the Operation Order," announced the brigadier. "Reference Maps ———"

I have a theory that, while the battles the British fight may differ in the widest possible way, they have invariably two common characteristics—they are always fought uphill and always at the junction of two or more map sheets.

This battle was to be no exception. The brigadier named four separate sheets of the one-inch map, and you are to imagine half a dozen field officers in a restricted space, each trying to fit together four large squares of paper. Some seated themselves and tried to spread them over their knees, some to hold them against the wall. My colonel carpeted the ground with his and used them much as a devout Mohammedan uses his prayer-mat. There was such a rustling, flapping, and crackling, such an undertone of cursing, that we missed the paragraph of the order headed, *"Information, our own and enemy forces."*

However, we did find Panch Pir, a couple of tiny red squares on the map about eleven miles south of us as the crow flies, but a good deal farther by the only practicable route.

---

[5] *Unofficial History,* David McKay, New York, 1962, p. 104.

Unhappily for the western world, the Germans during World War I, throughout the interwar period, and well into World War II continued to devote their formidable energies to theoretical as well as practical aspects of warfare. They did not neglect war games and other related exercises.

Indeed, by the early days of the twentieth century, there were several such German activities other than the war game proper,[6] the purpose of which was to train all ranks in reaching decisions as to objectives in war, and in issuing orders for the purpose of accomplishing those objectives. The proper war game was always at least two-sided (if allies were involved, more than two parts could be played) and under control of a game director, or umpire. But the generic term "war game" covered, and still covers: the map exercise, conducted by a director and one side only for the purpose of training players in tactical concepts; the staff exercise, another one-party device for the education of staff officers in their functions; the training trip, an extended exercise accomplished in the field as either a war game proper or a map exercise; the tactical walk, carried out in the field within narrow tactical limits in order to train participants for the command of small military units; the command-post exercise (CPX in American military usage), designed to employ communications systems and to familiarize commanders and staffs with the command and control system required in meeting an assumed situation; the special exercise, used for numerous purposes, each of a specific nature, such as to test the operation of a supply system, or of a new weapon, or of a new type of military organization; and the sand-table exercise, employed for the indoor tactical

[6] Hofman, Rudolf, General der Infanterie, Department of Army, Office of the Chief of Military History, *War Games*, MS P-094 draft translation, Washington, D.C., 1952, pp. 1–5.

training of very small units. Field exercises or maneuvers employing actual troops fall beyond the scope of our present interest.

The projected offensive of the German Army for the spring of 1918 was played out in advance, as a strategic war game, at the Army Group Headquarters of Crown Prince Rupprecht.[7] In consequence, it became apparent to the German Army High Command that the chances of marked success for this operation were exceedingly slight. While the offensive was nevertheless mounted, it probably was at least partially as a result of this game that the attack was not pressed to the point at which the German Army might have disintegrated in the field. It is a verdict of history that the ordered withdrawal and surrender of German arms later in the year permitted the notion to persevere, in Germany, that it was not a failure of the army, but of civilian support, that accomplished German defeat. There thus was laid one of the significant bases for a rapid resurgence of German arms under Hitler. Germans, whether military or civilian, retained full faith in the superiority of their military tradition and prowess.

There was another important reason why Hitler was able so rapidly to reconstitute the German military machine. The few officers permitted to the reduced German Army after Versailles felt there was no choice, in training and planning for an expansion, but to resort to every means of simulating forces, weapons, and field maneuvers. They were driven to map maneuvers and war games for the practical training of troop units, as well as for the examination, at command levels, of strategic possibilities. Efforts were made to study the military problems that Germany might, in the new circumstances, encounter on its borders. In addition, through

[7] *Ibid.*, pp. v–vi.

games and map exercises, especially under Field Marshal von Blomberg, progress was made in reaching an understanding of the requirements for achieving cooperation among the High Command, the Army, the Navy, and the Air Force.

It must be conceded that the results of such work were not always convincing. As World War II approached, Hitler indicated his "unalterable decision to destroy Czechoslovakia in the immediate future in a military operation."[8] Colonel General Beck, as Chief of Staff, used the results of a relevant map maneuver to buttress his argument that the proposed operation was unsound, because of the tragedy that would follow for Germany as well as for the rest of Europe. In the short term, he was spectacularly wrong. But even Hitler might later have found him right.

German commanders during the period of the "Phony War," after the blitz of Poland and while preparing for the 1940 assault against western Europe, used the time to great advantage with a series of map games and exercises. Having breached the Maginot Line, the Wehrmacht was able to exploit its success on an unprecedented scale as, with a precision deriving in large part from detailed map rehearsals, it swept to the Channel within weeks and forced the withdrawal of metropolitan France from the war. Here is a description of the planning involved:[9]

> . . . the Army High Command was chiefly occupied with the problem as to where the main force of the first offensive thrust was to be directed and how the obstacle of the Ardennes was to be overcome by large motorized units.
>
> For this purpose the Army High Command held war

[8] Hofman, Rudolf, *op. cit.,* pp. 29–30.
[9] *Ibid.,* pp. 31–33.

games lasting for several days under the direction of the Assistant Chief of Staff I, General von Stuelpnagel, as well as a map exercise also lasting several days under the Chief of Operations Branch. Both exercises were held in the headquarters in Zossen and were supplemented by trips along the border taken by the Army Chief of Staff.

. . . The exercises were based on the German operational plans and the enemy situation as it was known at the time. . . . The purpose of this theoretical exercise was not to carry out our operational drafts in the form of war games, but rather to provide a possibility for raising and discussing controversial problems within an especially selected and critical circle. Therefore, the exercise did not proceed in the form of a continuous game, but rather in "bounds," in which connection the situations which were probably to be expected were represented anew on each occasion. The lessons learned during the game were evaluated by General von Stuelpnagel in a report to the Chief of Army Staff, Generaloberst Halder. . . .

. . . The map exercise . . . was intended to check whether the possibility and time allowance for traversing the Ardennes with armored units, as estimated by the Chief of Staff, could with a certain degree of probability prove correct. All available German and Belgium maps, as well as aerial photographs of the terrain, were used as a basis for the exercises; the field units had to report the exact figures and march spaces of all the units involved down to the individual repair shop trucks. The executive positions of all units were filled by officers from the General Staff and the technical troops. The capacity of the roads, secondary routes and parking places assigned to them had to be entered in small-scale maps in such a way as to give a cartographically correct picture of where the columns and individual vehicles were located at any time with due regard for their security distances and the intervals between march units. This "test" was repeated by the directors every six hours, and each time it was ascertained when, where and what kind of interruptions might be expected as the result of enemy action, traffic congestion, refueling and the condition of the roads. This map study, therefore, was based largely on mathematical calculations, and these calculations were in turn largely based on earlier experience gained by the armored troops in peacetime and during the Polish campaign. Actual events showed the troops covered the distances assigned to them more quickly than had been estimated . . . probably because the French and Belgian air forces did not prove as effective as had been feared. . . .

. . . Both the war game and the map exercise gave the Chief of Staff useful information for his final plan of operation; and he was able to supplement this information by personal trips to the border area and by participating in the operation games held. . . .

However, for an example of sheer professionalism, nothing surpasses the opportunistic attitude of Field Marshal Model in early November 1944.[10] It was the eve of the Battle of the Bulge. The staff of the Fifth Panzer Army was rehearsing defensive measures against an American attack that might, it was thought, be aimed at the juncture of the Fifth and Seventh Armies. In the midst of the map exercise, the Americans commenced an attack in the Hurtgen-Gemeter area similar to the one postulated. Model, under whose direction the map rehearsal was taking place, promptly ordered that the game continue, but on the basis of actual combat reports. The map exercise was thus merged with, and evolved into, command during wartime, with, it might be said, very good results for the Wehrmacht.

[10] Hofman, Rudolf, *op. cit.,* pp. 19–20.

Chapter III

COUSINS OF CRISIS GAMING

A number of present activities, including crisis gaming, are related to the war games that were quite fully developed before the close of the nineteenth century. The closest relationship is that of current war games. Next closest, perhaps, is the gaming technique sometimes employed in analyzing business operations. Second-cousins-once-removed are the several political exercises. In this chapter we shall touch lightly on the crisis game's principal existing cousins. These include computer war gaming, business or management gaming, behaviorist simulation of international relations, and the construction of alternative futures.[1]

---

[1] The omission of game theory is deliberate. The theory of games is a branch of mathematics which deals with a kind of tacit bargaining between two or more people who must choose among a number of alternatives at the same time and without consulting each other. Their choices mesh in such manner as to cause numerically expressed gains and losses. Game theory has in common with life an important situation in which both or all may gain, not necessarily equally, by agreeing on certain choices. If the many values, choices, alternatives, and contingencies of political conflict problems could be given valid numerical weights, game theory would contribute enormously to their solution. It seems doubtful that this can be done, however, until, in a phrase from the elegant repertoire of Nikita Khrushchev, shrimps learn to whistle. To suggest that current game theory can contribute importantly to solving international conflict is about the same as suggesting that the best way to catch a bird is to put salt on its tail. A succinct introduction to game theory is contained in Kaplan, Morton A., *System and Process in International Politics*, New York, John Wiley & Sons, Inc., 1957.

Computer war gaming. Ground and naval warfare, more than air warfare, continue to rely on manually played games, but most of the specific operations of fighting forces, whether in logistics, intelligence, communications, or command, receive a considerable exposure to computers. This exposure may not always result in a game; that is, a contest. An operation, such as the movement of forces by air, can be simulated on a computer after a model has been developed to represent interacting parts of the operation. Clark C. Abt says: "War games are sometimes confused with models and simulations, since sometimes models are 'gamed,' games are modeled, and both models and games are simulated. A *game* is any contest played according to rules and decided by skill, strength, or apparent luck. A *model* is a representation—actual or theoretical—of the structure or dynamics of a thing in process. A *simulation* is an operating imitation of a real process."[2]

The prime characteristic of the model designed for the computer is that it faithfully reflects the rules and decisions of the modelmaker. In order to develop these, the modelmakers first have to think through, or manually play through, sequences of military operations. On the basis of a mathematical language adapted to the computer, this vision of what would or could happen in various circumstances is introduced as data and instructions into the computer's storage system, or memory. Although even an advanced computer is a simple-minded beast, its memory, speed, and patience allow it to handle problems the complexities of which are limited only by the ingenuity of the programmers.

Consider for computer treatment a fragment of an air

[2] "War Gaming," *International Science and Technology,* August 1964, p. 29.

battle, in which a single bomber is ordered to take off, refuel in flight, penetrate hostile defenses, attack a specified target, and then return to a recovery base. Does the bomber take off in time? This may be the function of a series of yes-no questions concerning reliability of communications, security of the bomber's base, whether the bomber is in commission, etc. Does the refueling occur on schedule? Again a series of questions, this time related to the performance of the tanker aircraft, accuracy of rendezvous, success in coupling, etc. Is penetration successful? Here we can expect that the series of yes-no answers proceeds primarily from a stochastic, or probabilistic, process which the machine employs according to instructions it has received, perhaps on the basis of selecting random numbers. Probabilities will be based on assumptions or experience concerning per cent of failure (or success) of the enemy air defenses against bomber penetrations. Does the bomber find its target? Again, a series of yes-no questions, attuned perhaps to possible radar failure, navigational error, weather conditions, etc. Are "bombs away" at the correct bomb release line? Another series of yes-no questions. Does the aircraft return successfully? More of the same.

The computer programmer would describe the bomber operation in a flow diagram like the simplified one in Figure 1. (Its final box encompasses the action following a successful penetration.)

Performance of the bomber in this situation could be analyzed by hand. Then why resort to the computer? Because we wish to examine a series of related situations, from which we may glean very important information. The great value of the computer, even for the simple operation outlined above, is that *it permits repetition in which the effects of variables can be observed.* The flight profile of the bomber

43

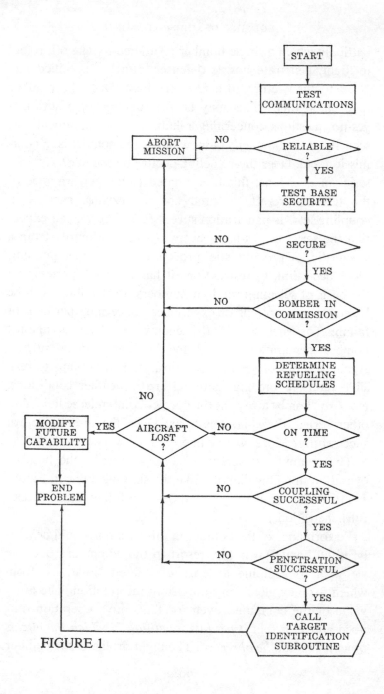

FIGURE 1

can be varied, for example, and by running through a series of altitudes for the final approach to the target we may discover one approach consistently more successful against the enemy defenses than others, thus materially cutting our probable losses. In planning actual combat operations, a single computer might therefore be worth dozens of bombers.

It will be seen from the table in Figure 2, taken from Livermore's *American Kriegsspiel* of 1882, that his calculations show an amusing as well as a startling resemblance to contemporary model building for computer war games. It is ap-

FIGURE 2
POSSIBILITY OF FIRING

		Kind of Troops	3 in.	R. C.	Mit.	Inf.
	(a) Power of Firing. Ammunition.	Scores on Small block	—	—	60	5
		Scores on Large block	6	2	6	½
		Min. of Com. Fire	120	40	30	25
Troops Firing.	(b) Organization.	Recently disp. check upon block. Temp. disp. check before the block.		No fire. If attacked.		
	Format. Position.	Col...Line...Sk...Dct...Firing...Ln. Cavalry Dismount. Artillery Unlimber.		¼ Min. or more. ½ Min. or 1 Min.		
	Previous Fire.	Range in as many min. as 1000 yds. less Rev. Can. ¼ as many as 1000 yds. less		Pips of Die. Pips of Die.		
Local Relations.	(c) Village.	Wooden. Only 1 man to 2½ yds. Stone. Only 1 man to 2½ yds. Surrounding walls. No fire over. After extinguishing flames. No fire.		For 2 Min. For 40 Min. For 20 Min. For 10 Min.		
	(d) Forest.	Only 2 men in 2½ yds. can fire to advantage. No distant fire in dense forest.				
	(e) Fortification.	Set forw. Min. Mk. if working parties fire. Only 2 men in 2½ yds. of crest can fire.				
	(f) Elevation. (g) Conceal. (h) Protect'n.	Inf. in line only 10°. Art. without preparation, 6°. If last part of descent steeper. Troops concealed. If No. of 10′ Curves in 40 yds. greater than No. of thousand yards in distance, Troops protected.				
	(i) No. of Yds.	1 score=20 yds.				
Weather, etc.	(j) Night. Rain. Fog. Wind.	Can see only 300 yds. ½ effect. Can see only as far as umpire permits. (Throw die.) Can see only as far as umpire permits. Effect on dust, smoke, etc.				

parent that the table could yield a series of yes-no questions for a digital computer. Under his category (b), are the troops in column, in line, as skirmishers, detached? Is the cavalry mounted or dismounted? Is the artillery unlimbered, and hence in firing position? Are the troops in a village? Yes or no. If yes, is the village built of wood or stone? If no, are the troops in a forest? If yes, only two men for each two and one-half yards of front can fire effectively, and distant fire is ineffective: the computer can be programmed to handle matters accordingly. When we get to category (j), we find a probabilistic element introduced with the throw of a die, and there are also umpire decisions suggested that, in a computer, could easily be handled by stochastic means.

The all-computer game is wholly rigid, for even the probabilistic element has been determined by the programmer in advance. The output, or print out, of any specific datum for a series of games in which the only variation results from probabilistic processes will be in the form of a curve. One could not predict the outcome of any particular run of the simulation, except that it would fall on a predictable curve.

The making of models for various types of gaming connected with the operations of military forces is a reasonably big business to which many specialists devote concentrated attention. Thus the Raytheon Company has been developing, under the supervision of Clark C. Abt,[3] a computer simulation of cold war and limited war for the Joint War Games Agency of the Joint Chiefs of Staff. An ambitious attempt has here gone into gaming political, economic, and psychological events, among other things, for as many as thirty-nine nations simultaneously. The designers do not

[3] *Op. cit.* This article contains reference to a number of recent or ongoing war games.

claim predictive capabilities for their model, known as TEMPER. They hope, however, to achieve good qualitative results on the basis of alternative assumptions, providing material for further analysis.

Reserve in claims for the computer simulation of any approach to total interactions among nations appears definitely in order. The mass of data for a realistic simulation would reach unmanageable proportions, even if it were all known and understood, so that very broad "givens" must be accepted. However, the notion of "all other things being equal" has to be taken with a whole pinch of salt. Henry M. Wriston, in retiring as president of the Council on Foreign Relations, observed that his father graduated in the second class of a university which in due course celebrated its centennial. His own alma mater, from which he, himself, had graduated in the initial class, at the same time celebrated its 102nd anniversary. All other factors being equal, Dr. Wriston pointed out, this could make him older than his father. (As it happens, his own institution had adopted the traditions, including the founding date, of a predecessor institution.)

Technical Operations Incorporated has developed for the U.S. Air Force, under Project Omega, a collection of simulation models for the study of air war, and air and missile battle models are employed by planners within Air Force Headquarters in the Pentagon.

The impressive U.S. Navy automated gaming at Newport is best described by Francis J. McHugh:[4]

> The Navy Electronic Warfare Simulator (NEWS) is a large and complex system that was designed and constructed for the express purpose of providing students of the Naval War College with the ". . . opportunity to gain

[4] *Fundamentals of War Gaming*, Naval War College, 1961, p. 5–1.

significant combat experience in a realistic setting and under the press of real time." It is, essentially, a two-sided . . . electro-mechanical war gaming device which enables the players to make command decisions at real-world or faster than real-world time, and which—subject to umpire control—automatically monitors and evaluates pertinent aspects of the employment and interactions of opposing forces.

The computer simulation of ground warfare, except where the encounter resembles a duel, as in a brush between tank and anti-tank weapons, is especially difficult. Methods for the design and operation of simulations involving ground combat are described in *Simulation Using Digital Computers* by G. W. Evans II, G. F. Wallace, and G. L. Sutherland.[5]

Business games.[6] Business or management gaming is employed mainly for training purposes. It need not involve competition of the kind provided by opposing teams, but does require a series of decisions. While most business games could be played entirely by hand, computers are often of great assistance, especially where considerable data needs to be processed. The man-machine game is therefore by no means uncommon.

Implicit in the business game is the notion that the trained and experienced players or teams can approach optimum solutions. To the extent that this is true, business games are rule games, for the impact of experience is to provide a feel for principles, rules, and regulations. But few games of interest to top management could be entirely rigid. The games are accordingly often rigged to introduce unfamiliar situations with opportunities for player judgment.

[5] Prentice-Hall, Inc., Englewood Cliffs, N.J., 1965.
[6] This passage owes much to AMA Management Report Number 55, *Simulation and Gaming: A Symposium,* General Management Division, American Management Association, Inc., 1961.

The business exercise has much the same advantage over simulations of other social subjects that economics has over other social sciences; it has money as a measuring device—the score can be kept on an accounting basis.

There are doubtless rather more than a hundred different business games available for one purpose or another in the United States. The general top-management game is designed to be played by a team, to require the allocation of resources in order to show maximum returns, and to assure consideration of all principal functions or aspects of the business concerned. But games are also designed to concentrate on training for such specific operations as production, advertising, selling, or financing. The problems encountered within specific industries have also been dramatized in business games.

The American Management Association has developed its General Management Game to concentrate attention on what in the political context is often called "command and control." Very large numbers of players simulate the staff of a corporation in a situation demanding numerous decisions under the pressure of time. The result is to demand a division of labor, requiring a delegation of authority from the top and an acceptance of responsibility at middle levels of management. Inasmuch as this game trains its participants in internal administration, it is often described as a "bureaucratic" game.

One of the best-known business games is entirely manual and uses a playing kit. It was developed by McKinsey & Company and first published in *Harvard Business Review*, so that it is generally known as "the Harvard game." The players move symbols on a game board to represent their decisions concerning the use of salesmen, production, advertising, plant investment, prices, and the funding of research and development. An umpire, using a table of random numbers, determines the results of using resources for advertising and for research and development, and also allocates sales and decides when salesmen resign. The playing period simulates one business quarter, which, in most cases, allows time for decisions to have some impact; a considerable number of periods must be played through in order to provide for a feed-back of results from decisions of long-term character.

Like computer war games, business games, especially those employing mathematical models, demand that the problem be thought through before the model can be designed. Training objectives must be clearly drawn, the situation or case history well defined, all pertinent facets of information flow and decision processes covered, etc.

Behaviorist simulation of international relations.[7] As an aspect of behavioral science, the laboratory simulation of international relations has had a recent vogue of modest proportions, mostly at Northwestern University under the tutelage of Harold Guetzkow and Richard C. Snyder, but with a considerable assist from Richard A. Brody of Stanford University. The Northwestern vehicle is described as "an Inter-Nation Simulation." It employs a set of "nations," none of which pretends to be real, named Algo, Erga, Ingo, Omne, and Utro. This device is designed to free the players (principally undergraduates and bright high school seniors) from any notions they may have acquired concerning the behavior of actual nations, so that experimentation can proceed on an idealized footing.

[7] This passage is based, for the most part, on material contained in *Simulation of International Relations* by Harold Guetzkow et al., Prentice-Hall, Inc., Englewood Cliffs, N.J., 1963, and in Richard A. Brody's "Some Systemic Effects of the Spread of Nuclear Weapons," *The Journal of Conflict Resolution,* December 1963.

Each nation is provided a Central Decision Maker, an External Decision Maker, and an Internal Decision Maker. The first represents a chief executive, the second a foreign secretary, and the third a budget chief. The Central Decision Maker may be symbolic in that "validator satisfaction" can serve in his stead. "Validators" are the group or groups within the nation who put the chief executive in office and who may therefore remove him. Their attitude is determined by a point system deriving from the progress of the game and, at least in part, from prestige ratings given Erga (or Ingo, as the case may be) by such friends or rivals as Algo, Omne, and Utro. Each imaginary nation is provided a beginning capability, which of course is not the same for large and small nations, consisting of point values for economic assets and for existing military capacity. Productivity rates are also assigned. The nations are then required to allocate their resources to one end or another, as the play progresses, somewhat as in the game of Monopoly.

Crisis games, as we shall see, make little or no conscious effort to provide for the consideration of internal political factors, because the experienced participants in such exercises can be relied upon to allow for domestic constraints. Specific provision for "validators" to limit and control the student players can only be regarded as a wise, and even an essential, feature of the Northwestern simulation.

The student decision makers are free to settle on national objectives without the constraint of an initial set of international relations, for they receive no information concerning the history of their laboratory world. However, the resources provided are insufficient to permit the full satisfaction either of internal consumption wants or of very aggressive designs upon neighbors. It was sometimes said in the Pentagon during World War II that the business of its inmates, as they dealt with the several demanding theaters of the war, was the allocation of deficits. The Northwestern model is set up to require a similarly realistic attitude of the student decision makers. But the relation to reality stops right there, for the roles played by the participants are, designedly, those of themselves as individuals reacting to the developing situation. They are not required to assess the capabilities and probable reactions of other nations, as are the decision makers of an actual country.

The student decision makers have open to them the possibility of devoting all their resources to improving "their" country's standard of living, for example, although at the cost of accepting a dangerously feeble security posture. In one game, Algo, as a middle-size power, elected to do just that, and at the same time attempted to achieve security through the formation of mutual security pacts. Algo's determined moves in pursuit of this policy largely governed the course of subsequent events.

Northwestern's imaginary countries can make war or pursue peace. Wars can be general or limited. Arms races can occur. Foreign trade can be fostered and foreign aid sought or bestowed. Consideration can be given to international organization. "Summit" conferences are possible, although written communications are also available. Events, including random events, are reported for all participants by a "world press."

The purpose of this kind of simulation is to develop a supplementary means of teaching international relations and, perhaps more importantly, to provide a vehicle for research and experimentation in the field of international relations. The extent to which the purified air of an imaginary world with make-believe nations can further the first purpose may properly be left to the judgment of political scientists. Basic philosophical concepts, at least, must surely emerge. As to the second purpose, it appears doubtful that students will behave like nations with any greater fidelity than, in another behaviorist research activity, rats behave like people.

Certainly, rats *do* behave like people in a good many animal respects, and students can certainly mirror the policies and actions of nations where the factors involved are entirely clear. As an example of such a case, the Northwestern Simulation can be used to "test" the fact, which would be stated as an hypothesis, that *a security alliance tends to tighten as the threat it faces appears to increase, and to fall apart as the threat dissolves.* If the simulation provides for a security alliance, varies the apparent threat to the alliance between the limits of "great threat" and "little or no threat," and provides for minor but troublesome elements of discord within the alliance, then it can be expected that the students, who presumably are no fools, will produce a tight alliance in the one case and a faltering alliance in the other.

But the simulation would have to be gimmicked, or structured, to an extent that would virtually prejudge the result if the hypothesis to be tested were: *Rich or big nations extend material aid to poor or small nations.* There has of course been truth in this hypothesis lately: India and Indonesia, among other countries, have received help from both the United States and the Soviet Union at the same time. China, which is big and also poor, has graciously provided Tommy guns and the like to several small and poor African countries. But the context and the motives have to be pretty clearly understood; what we have here, which has not always occurred throughout history, may prove to be a special case.

A dilemma probably exists for the experimental simulators, therefore, in that facts of international life do not need to be validated, whereas an hypothesis that poses a genuine question is likely to be prejudged by its introduction as a programmed element in a simulation. Figure 3[8] can perhaps be taken as illustrating this dilemma. It tabulates the results of a questionnaire, distributed to seven "nations" in a simulation, in which each was asked to rate the other six "nations" in terms of "friendliness-unfriendliness." The seven nations constituted two opposing blocs: E, O, and Y, and A, I, U, and Z. The questionnaire posed a series of questions designed, on a scoring basis, to demonstrate the degree of hostility or friendship perceived by each of the seven in appraising each of the other six. Manipulation of the resulting figures produces two columns of scores. The left column lists the rank of members of the opposed bloc, all of whom rank higher on a hostility scale than any member of the alliance, the ranks for which are shown in the column on the right.

In other words, the students thought their allies were more friendly than their enemies. As someone said, if you introduce rabbits into a hat you should not be surprised at what comes out.

Alternative futures.[9] One of the entertaining devices of science fiction is the notion of "parallel worlds," worlds which coincide in time but which have a common history only up to a point. At RAND and more recently at the Hudson Institute, Herman Kahn and his colleagues have set about the writing of fictional world futures. Like the scenarios used in politico-military games, as will be seen in Chap-

---

[8] Reproduced with permission from the Brody article previously cited.

[9] This passage is derived from Herman Kahn's *Alternative World Futures,* Document HI-342-B IV, Hudson Institute, April 1964, and from discussions at the Hudson Institute.

ter V, the Kahn future worlds describe possible situations without pretending that they are probable situations. Unlike the scenarios of politico-military games, which ought to be held to short-term futures, alternative futures attempt to deal with possibilities ten or more years hence. Except in a gross sense, prediction is not intended or attempted: Herman Kahn owns a fertile imagination but no crystal ball.

FIGURE 3

PERCEPTIONS OF INTER-BLOC AND INTRA-BLOC HOSTILITY

INTER-BLOC DYADS			INTRA-BLOC DYADS		
Dyad	Score	Rank	Dyad	Score	Rank
1. AE	230	27.5	1. AI	162	11
2. AO	229	26	2. AU	169	13
3. AY	234	29	3. AZ	178	18
4. EA	225	25	4. EO	134	2
5. EI	224	23.5	5. EY	149	7
6. EU	252	37	6. IA	160	10
7. EZ	239	33	7. IU	171	15
8. IE	224	23.5	8. IZ	165	12
9. IO	268	40	9. OE	151	8
10. IY	238	31.5	10. OY	142	5
11. OA	186	19	11. UA	177	17
12. OI	238	31.5	12. UI	139	3
13. OU	285	42	13. UZ	141	4
14. OZ	251	36	14. YE	144	6
15. UE	237	30	15. YO	124	1
16. UO	277	41	16. ZA	170	14
17. UY	259	39	17. ZI	173	16
18. YA	195	20	18. ZU	152	9
19. YI	222	22		$\Sigma = \overline{171} = R_1$	
20. YU	246	35			
21. YZ	242	34			
22. ZE	218	21			
23. ZO	254	38			
24. ZY	230	27.5			
	$\Sigma = \overline{732} = R_2$				

Each group of alternative futures—and the Hudson Institute has produced several—is based upon a model, or paradigm, that in a simplified but explicit manner develops a set of assertions, definitions, assumptions, conjectures, analyses, etc., about a world of the 1970s. A number of alternative futures are then constructed as they might come to occur under the conditions of the paradigm.

Thus Kahn has developed paradigms, classified by Greek letters, for worlds that: are "mostly peaceful and prosperous" (Alpha); possess "many structural stresses" (Beta); are characterized by "extensive multipolarity" (Gamma); revert to a situation of "containment and confrontation" (Delta); witness "Communism on the march" (Epsilon); see the "collapse of Europe" (Eta); see the "collapse of the third world" (Zeta); and several others. Each Alpha, Beta, or Zeta paradigm provides essential information for the development of the various explicit scenarios to be developed from it. Under Alpha, for example, the Soviet Union is "relatively rich, relatively relaxed, ideologically discouraged, highly deterred. Western Europe is united (including Britain), growing fast. China is growing slack. Japan is vigorous, armed. Third areas relatively calm, achieving moderate growth rates. U.S., U.S.S.R., Western Europe announce a no-cities nuclear policy."

Alpha 2 builds on these stated conditions a world in which Japan, while remaining vigorous and armed, is quiet, prosperous, constructive, and feels itself unthreatened, while Communist China has agreed to avoid war in return for extensive Soviet economic aid. Anyone for Alpha 2?

Another Alpha world, however, makes a bad actor out of Japan, and further changes are subsequently rung on the basic Alpha theme, as well of course as on the themes, Beta to Lambda.

There emerges from all of this a reasonably coherent set of possible futures which, without including all possibilities, may well come close to describing the limits of change in one direction and another. After all, ten years plus is not a long enough period in human affairs to produce radical change in most solidly established institutions. Another Hitler could revolutionize the policy of a major country, it is true, but China and India will surely continue to have population problems; Christianity, Islam, and Communism will surely continue to influence most of the world; and advanced weapon systems will not be expunged from the knowledge of men, though the control of such systems may conceivably develop. Some genuinely "permanent operating factors" will continue to operate, such as the influences of climate and geography. There are, in other words, a number of quite reliable reference points upon which to hang conjectures about the future, and these are considered in constructing the scenarios for alternative futures.

A sheaf of scenarios fanning out to cover the likely, and some of the unlikely, "worlds" of the 1970s ought, in the 1960s, to provide good value for planners in either government or industry. They might well place their own weights on the various alternative worlds, considering some more probable than others. But certainly, if the conditions or requirements of any considerable number of alternative futures are such that specific preparations may be adopted (and perhaps later adapted) to deal with any or all of them at the same time, the job of planning to meet the future is made that much simpler and that much surer. At the least, contingencies will be envisaged that should be worked for or, perhaps, guarded against.

Chapter IV

THE ADVENT OF POLITICO-MILITARY GAMING

The "politico-military," "cold war," or—in the form I prefer to give emphasis—"crisis" game is a direct outgrowth of free Kriegsspiel. So obvious is the transition that one can feel only surprise that its application had to await the period after World War I. A century earlier Clausewitz had already made it clear that war and politics were sides of a coin. If international politics might on occasion be considered without thought of war, war patently could never be considered without thought of politics. Clausewitz said that:

> . . . war belongs not to the province of the arts and sciences but to that of social existence. It is a conflict of great interests which is settled by bloodshed, and only in that is it different from other conflicts. It would be better, instead of comparing it to any art, to compare it to trade, which is also a conflict of human interests and activities; and it is much more like politics, which again, for its part, may be regarded as a kind of trade on a large scale. Furthermore, *politics is the womb in which war is developed,* in which its outlines lie hidden in a rudimentary state, like the qualities of living creatures in their embryos.[1]

Very probably the first significant political-military game was played in Germany during 1929. Erich von Manstein of the Army Staff had been given the task of organizing a war

---

[1] Clausewitz, *op. cit.,* p. 85. My italics. It might be hoped also that politics is the womb in which war is *not* developed.

game envisaging a Polish attack against East Prussia or Upper Silesia. In the circumstances, the notion that the Germans could actually fear Polish aggression is understandable, for Germany continued to be restricted by the Treaty of Versailles to an army of 100,000 men. The Poles—allied to the French and Czechs—in truth had the Germans outnumbered.

General Manstein says in his memoirs[2] that it seemed possible to him at the time that increasing political tension could lead to a Polish attack on East Prussia or Upper Silesia. Manstein felt that the Germans could not expect intervention by the League of Nations if Polish military moves were so rapid and decisive as to present the League with a *fait accompli*. Germany, on its part, would have to prevent such a result while also avoiding any move which France or Czechoslovakia could construe as requiring them to join the war against Germany as Polish allies. Manstein therefore proposed that the war game proper should follow upon a political exercise designed primarily for the wider education of both military and political leaders. This was done, with the result, as reported by Manstein, "that the gentlemen from the Foreign Office, to whom such a playing through of possible conflicts appeared to be quite new, enthusiastically appreciated the value of this approach."

We, however, may adopt a somewhat more skeptical attitude, especially in light of a later, and historically more important, effort of this type. This was the massive politico-military exercise played out in Tokyo during August 1941, under the auspices of a Total War Research Institute founded the previous year by the Japanese Government.[3]

[2] *Aus einem Soldatenleben,* Bonn, 1958, pp. 131–32.
[3] Exhibits 868 and 871 in *Tokyo War Crime Trial Documents,* Vol. 16.

The exercise was instrumental in determining certain courses of Japanese action, primarily the decision on expansion to the southeast; and at least one of the domestic policies instituted in the game, involving economic controls, was subsequently placed in effect by the Imperial Government.

In her analysis of events leading to Pearl Harbor,[4] Roberta Wohlstetter makes it plain that there were serious miscalculations of intent on the part of both the United States and Japan. Information was generally available, but officials of neither country could achieve any real empathy with those of the other, and intentions were accordingly often misread. Mrs. Wohlstetter makes the comment:

> This inability to imagine enemy psychology and tactics is, of course, a flaw inherent in most war games; the strategies are as good as the players and, on the whole, are typical of the players rather than of their identities in the game. The American decision makers, it has been noted, were rather poor at imagining Japanese intentions and Japanese values. It should be said that the Japanese themselves had essential difficulties . . . with projecting American responses to Japanese acts. Most unreal was their assumption that the United States, with ten times the military potential and a reputation for waging war until unconditional victory, would after a short struggle simply accept the annihilation of a considerable part of its air and naval forces and the whole of its power in the Far East.

The Tokyo game apparently afforded a clear demonstration of the inability, or the unwillingness, of the Japanese to cope with American thinking. It seems likely that unwillingness was the real problem. The Army representatives in the

[4] Wohlstetter, Roberta, *Pearl Harbor: Warning and Decision*, Stanford University Press, Stanford, Calif., 1962. Especially pp. 354–56.

1941 Tokyo game played a major—perhaps predominant— role in its direction. These officers were thoroughly familiar with the then current predictions of their service concerning the probable course of a future war in the Far East. As the play of the game developed a hot, if hypothetical, war as far into the future as 1943, the pattern was found to match co- zily the fixed predictions of the Army High Command. There was no mention, incidentally, of a possible strike against Pearl Harbor; if the Navy players knew it was under consideration, they may have regarded it as too sensitive a subject for discussion in the presence of Army and For- eign Office participants.

One interesting aspect of the Tokyo game was the extent to which the cast of home-team players reflected that historic conflict among various Japanese factions which had to be reconciled if, in the actuality, any meaningful actions were to be taken. Whether war had to occur, when it might occur, how it might commence, the probable composition of an enemy alliance, and what, if anything, Japan should confide to its own possible allies were all matters in debate. A con- siderable number of friendly and hostile nations were repre- sented, the European Axis powers as one, and, separately, the United States, Great Britain, the Soviet Union, China, Korea, Manchuria, Thailand, French Indochina, and the Netherlands East Indies.

It would be difficult to argue with Mrs. Wohlstetter that this exercise was really a game at all, in the sense of being an honest attempt to think competitively through a crisis situa- tion. It was rather a game played purposefully by the influ- ential Army clique as a means of persuading the Cabinet to adopt plans and premises favored by the Army. The protag- onists therefore were more the competing Japanese factions than the Japanese team and its potential foreign opposition.

61

Mrs. Wohlstetter says flatly: "This political game . . . does not seem to have been an actual testing of alternatives, but rather a sophisticated way of demonstrating or arguing a set of convictions. The favorable prognosis for the Japanese forces, as well as the vagueness with which the outcome of American and British opposition was handled, bears a close relation to the actual arguments presented to the Emperor by General Sugiyama, the Army Chief of Staff."

Turning now to one of Japan's close neighbors, the record is clear that the Soviet armed forces, like those of other powers, do employ war gaming as a tool for planning and training. Whether the Soviet Union, or Communist China for that matter, indulges in games having a political content we do not know. *The Sunday Times* of London carried a story on December 9, 1956, by an Alexander Metaxas, described as a "Russian-speaking French journalist recently back from the Soviet Union," to the effect that crisis gaming, or something akin to it, was of singular importance to the U.S.S.R.

"While the Western countries spend much of their intellectual energies on questions of internal politics," he wrote, "the Russians have trained their diplomatic investigators quietly but tenaciously—much, in fact, as their children are trained in schools established for that one purpose—to become the elite of the world's chess-players.

"Shepilov is a product of this system, a technician of that chess game for high stakes which is called Soviet diplomacy.

"The experts of the superior chess-club-*cum*-factory known as the Minindel, or Soviet Foreign Office, have their own way of dealing with any given situation. They take all the 'pros' and all the 'cons' and put themselves in the place of each interested party in turn. They draw up a list of all the possible eventualities. After pondering all the imponderables, they reach an almost mathematical degree of certainty about the course to be followed: and they follow it."

It might be added that they follow it with frequently poor results, assuming that the Russian master chess players of diplomacy whomped up in any such manner the calculations leading, for example, to the Cuban missile ploy or to the dissolution of a tidy Communist world centered on Moscow.

In fact, one is entitled to wonder whether doctrinaire officials, such as Communist true believers in the Soviet Union or the People's Republic of China, or even those not-so-true believers who are nevertheless compelled by the system to couch their efforts in terms of dogma, can ever achieve that pragmatic understanding of other peoples required for useful crisis gaming, or, in fact, for any perceptive analysis of international realities. George F. Kennan thinks not.

In everything that can be statistically expressed—expressed, that is, in such a way as not to imply any judgment on our motivation—I believe the Soviet Government to be excellently informed about us. I am sure that their information on the development of our economies, on the state of our military preparations, on our scientific progress, etc., is absolutely first-rate. But when it comes to the analysis of our motives, to the things that make our life tick as it does, I think this whole great system of intelligence-gathering breaks down seriously. It breaks down because over all these forty years the Communist party has made it impossible for the people who collect the factual information to accompany that information with any really objective analysis of the nature of Western society. Some of the fictions dearest and most basic to Russian Communism's view of itself would be jeopardized at every turn by that sort of analysis. The Soviet diplomatic representative or journalist abroad has no choice but to cast his analytical report in the terms of Marxist-Leninist ideology whether this is applicable or not in the given instance. In this way the Soviet leaders find themselves committed to a badly distorted image of the outside world.[5]

In the United States the RAND Corporation of Santa Monica, California, gets credit for pioneering the crisis game. Early RAND experimentation with the technique began during 1948 within the Mathematics Division, which is less surprising than it might appear: mathematicians are great hands at employing their craft in odd directions. At any rate, a series of three games was played out, extending into 1949 and involving three teams. The Blue team in accordance with custom represented the United States. The Red team represented Russia, which is probably never much annoyed by this color designation. There was also a team of umpires. In the first game the competing teams attempted to project ongoing cold war strategies. The second game was set forward to the year 1953 and assumed that Stalin was dead, the Soviet Union sometimes conciliatory, an Atlantic alliance in existence, and conflict pending because of a Soviet move in Scandinavia. The third play followed along analogous lines.

Efforts were then dropped until 1954, when the RAND Mathematics Division became concerned with building a computer model of a cold war game. This is of interest in the present connection in that officers of the Air War College at Maxwell Air Force Base, Alabama, became aware of the project, as also did personnel of the Department of State. Both the college, because of an interest in bomb-damage assessment, and the Department, for obvious reasons, wished to see political and economic factors entered into the starting model as well as into the evaluation phase. The interest

[5] *Russia, the Atom and the West,* Harper & Row, New York, 1957, p. 21 f.

64

of these agencies thereupon led into a new gaming effort to be described shortly.

In December 1954, then, a number of RAND economists and mathematicians, aided by a few social scientists, ran through a cold war game that was partly machine-played and partly hand-played.

In the meantime, RAND's Social Science Division began an independent series of experiments with what was called "political gaming," defined as a procedure for studying foreign affairs. The technique thus developed has in important respects been the prototype for succeeding American attempts to game out situations of conflict, whether international or otherwise. A central notion was to eliminate oversimplifications of international politics, such as had unavoidably been relied upon in the Mathematics Division, especially in the 1954 man-machine game, and to represent with as much fidelity as possible their genuine complexity.

The Social Science Division at RAND played four political games during 1955 and early 1956, successive games becoming lengthier and more heavily staffed. These games have been described by Herbert Goldhamer and Hans Speier,[6] who also make several significant points in their evaluation of the technique which I will touch upon at the close of this book.

Scenarios for the first three of these games began with actual events of the time; that is, no attempt was made to produce fictitious futures as the starting points for play. But this reportedly resulted in confusing game happenings with newspaper headlines. In some cases, the daily news apparently overtook developments in the games. The fourth game

6 "Some Observations on Political Gaming," *World Politics,* October 1959.

was therefore launched on the basis of a scenario describing events up to a point nine months later than the time it was written. All players were able to start on the common basis of this scenario and proceeded thenceforth without concern for the alarums and excursions of the workaday world.

Goldhamer and Speier say that the game was designed to meet these requirements:[7]

(1) *Minimal formalization.* Rules were non-existent. Rather, questions were subjected to discussion and exploration.

(2) *Simulation of contingent factors.* Chance, as well as matters beyond control of the nations portrayed, was introduced by having the umpiring team play the role of "Nature."

(3) *Plausibility of game events.* Implausible conduct was guarded against by the experience and judgment of the game participants.

(4) *Clarification of issues.* This was designed to be achieved in part by intramural team discussions, in part by the clarity of the scenarios, and in part through limitations on the number of players and emphasis upon their qualifications.

(5) *Exploration of novel strategies.* An attempt was made to require of the teams normal or "predicted" strategies (what the Soviet Union, for example, might be expected to do in terms of the record) and "optimal" strategies (what the United States might *best* do, in a given situation, regardless of constraints upon its actions deriving from the past record: for instance, the President may feel unable to make gestures toward Communist China strongly opposed by U.S.

---

[7] The italicized topic headings are taken from their article. I have paraphrased the original comment under these headings.

public opinion; this does not necessarily mean that he should not).

While the latest RAND approach was gestating, an ambitious "cold war" game was attempted under the aegis of the Air War College back in Alabama. My own interest in gaming began (sketchily) with this project, inasmuch as I reported for duty as Vice Commandant of the college in the fall of 1954—just as the players were folding their tents for home. This in many cases was Washington; a substantial number of the 100 or more participants came from the Department of State and the Pentagon. It was, and is, my impression that too many players were involved at too many odd intervals, for the practice was to bob in and out of a play which went on during two or three months. A laudable object of the game was to explore means by which U.S. air power might be applied, short of warfare, in order to influence aspects of the cold war favorably. As I recall, war kept breaking out nonetheless, for this was an innocent period when many thought war between the United States and the Soviet Union an acceptable alternative. It was necessary for the participants to fall out and regroup for a new start at intervals during the exercise.

The RAND experimentation became widely known in academic circles by 1959. Goldhamer and Speier[8] could report:

> In the summer of 1956, Hans Speier presented a summary of our experience as of that date to a Social Science Research Council summer institute in Denver, and in 1957 to the Fellows at the Center for Advanced Study in the Behavioral Sciences at Stanford. On several occasions during 1956–1958, Herbert Goldhamer lectured on the political

[8] *Op. cit.,* p. 80.

game at the Army War College, and Joseph Goldsen discussed it at faculty and student gatherings at Yale and at a conference sponsored by the Carnegie Endowment for International Peace at Princeton. Informal discussions about political gaming have been held with personnel of the Department of State, the Center for International Affairs at Harvard, the Brookings Institution, Northwestern University, and the Massachusetts Institute of Technology. In June 1959, the Social Science Research Council held a conference at West Point, N. Y., on teaching and research in the field of national security. At one of the sessions Hans Speier described the RAND experiments in political gaming, and several social scientists from various academic institutions . . . reported on their own experiences with such games. Finally, in September 1959, Herbert Goldhamer presented a paper on political gaming at the annual meeting of the Political Science Association in Washington, D.C.

A simplified form of political gaming was undertaken at M.I.T. during 1957–58 on the basis of a graduate seminar, players sitting around a table and making their moves orally. This was conducted by W. Phillips Davidson of RAND, then serving as a visiting professor. Subsequently, at M.I.T., Professors Lucian Pye and Warner Schilling used the technique, with variations, for a course in American diplomacy. Professor Norman J. Padelford later attempted games with M.I.T. undergraduates. But the flowering of the technique at M.I.T. has come under the tutelage of Professor Lincoln P. Bloomfield, who has pursued an extensive and purposeful course of political gaming, sometimes at M.I.T.'s Endicott House and sometimes in Washington. The Bloomfield games have involved a frequent employment of government players and have been designed (as in a series of "arms control" exercises devised for the Institute for Defense Analyses, in connection with a contract for the Department of Defense) to illumine questions of national policy.

As evidence of additional academic interest, there should be mentioned an ambitious undergraduate game instigated by Bernard C. Cohen[9] at the University of Wisconsin in the spring of 1960. This game involved ninety students over a two-week period, although prior preparation of student papers was also required. Eight countries in addition to the United States were represented, which should have introduced an ample amount of confusion (and did, according to Cohen). Political games have also been played on an undergraduate level at West Point and Columbia University.

The Stanford Research Institute during the past two or three years, under the leadership of George Evans of the Mathematical Sciences Department and James Adams of the Social Sciences Department, has shown a marked ability to generate crisis games as well as games dealing with such other forms of conflict as labor-management relations.

Beginning in 1961, the Joint Chiefs of Staff, through a subordinate element of the Joint Staff that later evolved into the Joint War Games Agency, embarked upon a series of "politico-military desk games." These games, like Bloomfield's M.I.T. games, have been directed at specific problems of national interest, and seem certain to carry for some time official classifications of security verging on the celebrated "One Eye Only; Destroy Yourself After Reading." However, there is happily available a published abstract on the subject having official blessing.[10]

[9] "Political Gaming in the Classroom," *The Journal of Politics*, May 1962.
[10] JCS Politico-Military Desk Games, presented by Lt. Col. Thomas J. McDonald, JWGA, Office of the Joint Chiefs of Staff, in *Second War Gaming Symposium Proceedings*, Washington Operations Research Council, 16, 17 March, 1964, p. 63.

[Politico-military] desk games are different from most games employed in operations research, particularly as they are played in the Joint Staff. In the Joint War Games Agency, these games are used to assist in the analysis of national objectives, policies, plans, programs, and organization by illuminating future possible contingencies. They are not intended to be predictive. They are played by top level officials from the White House, State and Defense Departments, and the Services for the following benefits: Simulated crises environment; realistic communications obstacles; exercise of command, control and intelligence systems; build interagency and interechelon rapport; point up weak spots in coordination, etc.; provide "feel" for Cold War "bargaining," negotiation, and escalation processes; broad overview for specialists; cross-fertilize ideas between agencies.

They are prepared in [the Joint War Games Agency] with help from interested agencies who contribute facts and ideas for scenarios, [and are] conducted in the Pentagon during four to six day sessions in which selected action officials from agencies meet several hours daily as Blue, Red and Control teams to devise strategies. Top senior officials meet for an hour each day to review and finalize decisions. Fact books, scenarios, messages and final critique [are] distributed afterward for analysis.

[These games are] also used in war colleges as an educational medium and in operations research for predicting possible future hardware requirements. . . .

Chapter V
CRISIS GAME TECHNIQUE

The preceding chapter suggests something of what crisis gaming is about. Specifically, the purpose is to achieve plausible simulations of possible international conflicts which the players ought then to resolve without either a compromise of vital interests or a resort to warfare. Difficult problems of international conflict do arise, of course, in which there is no threat of armed force. Great Britain's exclusion from the Common Market, caused in the first instance by British hesitations and then by the forthright veto of France, represents one such actual problem. But pretended situations of this less dramatic type will normally fail to command the efforts of people who are qualified to produce meaningful results in a game context. Scenarios that threaten collision courses capable of leading into disastrous warfare, on the other hand, are likely to enlist the active interest of responsible officials and other knowledgeable people.

Obviously, there is an assumption here that crisis game results *can* be meaningful: an evaluation of the utility of crisis gaming must await the conclusion of this book, when the reader will have had an explanation of the technique, with examples. Game technique needs now to be described.

The setting ranges from the barely adequate to the elaborate. A minimum setting depends in the first instance on the number of teams involved. Each team, including the Control team, requires a room capable of accommodating its members, and there is need also for a room to function as a message center. If the situation calls for only two independent teams, such as the United States and the Soviet Union, all other roles being played by the Control team, four rooms are needed. They need not be contiguous, but must be neighborly enough to permit ready communication, through the message center, between Control and each protagonist team. In addition, the group must have access to a conference or classroom that permits at least preliminary and concluding meetings of the entire cast; if any of the game rooms is large enough, it can double to satisfy this need.

Endicott House, at Dedham, Massachusetts, which has been used for a number of M.I.T.-sponsored games, is ideal for the purpose. The spacious residence not only provides ample facilities for the actual play of the game but can house most or all of the participants and provide meals and other essential refreshment. What makes this ideal is that players are sheltered from the interruptions and events of the real world and hence can the more easily be brought to concentrate on the make-believe. Professor Bloomfield reports one game in which the illusion of reality became so intense that the "Russian" team began to act as an inviolable unit even during recreation breaks, and before the play was concluded its members were patronizing the GENT's room in a body. Most campuses during off-term periods could provide something like Endicott House sequestration for game purposes.

The purpose of the message center is served if it is capable of recording and transmitting messages with speed and accuracy, of providing administrative services to the game participants, and of retaining (and duplicating) complete sets of game papers. It may also provide a convenient *ad hoc* meeting room, especially if equipped with a coffee machine.

The team and Control rooms should furnish conference-table space for all participants, necessary office equipment, means of displaying relevant maps and charts, and black-boards. Ample blackboard space is of great assistance in the formulation of agreed strategies, positions, actions, etc. Unless used for game purposes—which I will shortly discourage—telephones are best dispensed with.

Few, if any, crisis games thus far have placed any reliance on computers, but it seems probable that future games will come to rely on at least the computer processing of data bearing on the exercise. Special requirements in such a connection would presumably be determined by the physical location and environment of the automatic equipment.

Administrative support requirements have been indicated by Professor Bloomfield in connection with the M.I.T. exercises. There should be a Game Director, who might in a pinch serve also as Chairman of the Control team, an administrative assistant to the Game Director, two message-center clerks (graduate students, at M.I.T.), one typist per team, and a duplicating machine operator.

The starting scenario for each exercise is of prime importance in that it sets the stage for the entire play, which thereafter will be largely extemporized by the players. All too little difficulty exists in devising situations of conflict. In many cases they need not be devised at all, but rather an existing conflict carried, with a few sharp twists suggested by imagination and judgment, into the future. During a recent period of three months, the *New York Times* produced twenty-seven distinct reports of actual or potential armed conflict. Sample headlines:

73

CLASH REPORTED AT KASHMIR LINE
CYPRUS ACTION CAUSES STRAIN ON FAR-FLUNG BRITISH FORCES
FRENCH-AFRICAN BITTERNESS INCREASING IN GABON
CANAL ZONE RIOTING KILLS 2 STUDENTS
MALAYSIA WARNS ON AIR INTRUSIONS
IRAQI-KURD TRUCE BELIEVED FAILING
LAOS NEUTRALISTS SAY REDS ATTACK
8,000 WATUSIS REPORTED SLAIN IN TRIBAL STRIFE
KENYA POLICE TO OUST AFRICANS
RED CHINA CHARGES INDIA INCITES TIBET
ETHIOPIA CHARGES TRUCE IS BROKEN
SYRIA REVOLT REPORTED GROWING
BELGRADE ACCUSES BULGARIANS OF STIRRING MACEDONIA ISSUE

This ought to be enough to convey the idea, without mentioning headlines concerned with the Congo, South Vietnam, Cuba, Berlin, South Korea, or Taiwan.

For best effect the scenario has to project a situation far enough in the future to assure that game events will not become ensnarled, because too similar, with the news of the day. However, it must also avoid moving so far ahead that it outruns the capacity of the players to conceive a consistent future. After all, in most games it will prove impracticable to provide, or to assimilate, more than a minimum of artificial background material—normally, just sufficient to make the simulated situation plausible in the setting of the real world, most of which has to be conceived as little changed from what the players know of it. The ecology, in effect, has to be held still while some of its associated organisms are made to wriggle. In this respect, game scenarios differ sharply from the diverting type of science fiction that poses familiar microcosms in a wholly changed environmental macrocosm.

74

In order to provide the participants with a launching platform for their joint venture into the future, a "fact book" can be assembled (as it is, most expertly, in Pentagon games) to cover, *inter alia,* ethnic, economic, geographical, and historical matters having an important bearing on the game problem. This serves to assure the players a common understanding of the real world, very helpful to their simulation of an unreal one. But maps, yearbooks, an encyclopedia, and perhaps some published articles and area studies can be assembled to serve the same end.

Scenarios can be devised to fit special purposes. For example, scenarios have been drawn to permit explorations of separate simultaneous guerrilla warfare situations that might have the consequence of stretching the military capabilities of one major protagonist. Scenarios have been written to provide paper tests for the employment of various assumed international forces. Arms control problems have also been examined on a gaming basis. Despite their frequently useful results, such games are inhibited to the extent that the team players are constrained by their instructions, or by the actions of Control, to remain faithful to some special research purpose. For crisis gaming purposes, the preference should go to proceeding where logic and fancy may lead.

Excessive emphasis need not be placed on writing scenarios which, because they are so closely extrapolated from history and current events, arouse protest from no one. The situations thus developed will be long on plausibility, but are likely to be short on interest. One should shoot for the contriving of situations, rather, that call for new policies and new actions, and in fact a rethinking of policy stances which, however hallowed by custom, will not fit a changed world. Herman Kahn and Irwin Mann,[1] speaking of war gaming, make the apt observation: "It is true that one way a situation can be interesting is because it is probable, but it is also true that relatively improbable situations are very interesting because if they occur they are so extraordinarily important. . . . the game should be guided into a study of situations about which one wishes to be educated and not simply because one thinks they are most likely to happen." In point of fact, improbable things happen in international politics with alarming consistency.

Particularly in confrontations, as between the United States and the Soviet Union or the United States and Communist China, it is preferable that at least some part of the starting scenario be written in two versions to reflect differing views of the same events. Here it will prove easy to write the U.S. view of events leading to the crisis, but some skill and insight will be needed in seeing the situation and its antecedents through one or another pair of pink glasses. And there is also utility in adding or subtracting from the information available to one side in providing information to the other. In the real world, intelligence is sketchily available and what is known can be misinterpreted. (The simulation of intelligence is one of the most difficult problems in crisis gaming and probably—measurement is impossible—failure in this respect introduces more error than failure of any other kind.) Where divergent scenarios are employed, each contesting team should of course be shown only the version tailored to its own presumed knowledge and bias.

The starting scenario has to be tailored in another fashion as well, this time to fit the manner in which moves of the game are scheduled. If, as is often convenient, the moves

[1] *War Gaming*, p. 1167, The RAND Corporation, 1957.

of playing teams are to take place simultaneously, the initial situation has to be set up so as to demand decisions and actions from each principal team by the close of the first team move period. Where the players are sequestered, as at Endicott House, simultaneous moves are likely to be essential for orderly management. However, a somewhat more realistic pattern of moves is possible when play of the game is less concentrated, especially when the players are devoting part-time to the exercise. Team moves can be scheduled for alternate periods, and even on alternate days. One team can be presented with the requirement to take action on a situation raised by the starting scenario, while the remaining teams go about other affairs. Their subsequent reactions fuel the problem to require a second response from the first team. A "shoelace" pattern of play then emerges, as will be illustrated in the next chapter.

The players can be, and generally are, selected from among intermediate-rank officials to fit the problem under consideration in a Washington game, which is likely to differ from other games in the additional matter of distinguishing between seniors and staff. Very high officials of the government, to include Cabinet officers and members of the Joint Chiefs of Staff, have been persuaded to participate in Pentagon exercises. Because of their intense schedules, however, they have been brought in only briefly, in order to make judgments as senior members of teams composed primarily of full-time working staffs. Meetings of seniors and staffs occur for perhaps no more than an hour each day, usually prior to lunch because this fits conveniently both with VIP schedules and the pattern of game moves.

Games conducted under academic auspices provide an opportunity to blend town and gown with mutual profit, although visitors can also be invited in; foreign visitors might on occasion make especially noteworthy contributions. In most cases, the college or university is likely to have attracted to its vicinity a number of former foreign service officers, ex-aid administrators, retired military, naval, and air force officers, etc. Drafted, along with senior faculty members, to fill out the cast of gamers, such people can provide a useful leaven of recent practical experience plus necessary expertise in areas of importance to any crisis game. These areas, in addition to regional specialization, are primarily diplomatic and military.

Teams having major parts to play need about five players. More will prove unwieldy, and less make it difficult to provide for specialties and to get the work done. The Game Director should appoint one player as Chairman of each team, including the Control team, after which the teams should be allowed to organize themselves to fit their own concepts of the roles they will play. Experience suggests that each Chairman should appoint a military player as well as a diplomatic player, for the games almost inevitably demand consideration of military postures and threats. Walt W. Rostow is persuasive on this point:[2] "There is hardly a diplomatic move we make in the contemporary world which does not raise the question, does the US have the capability and the will to back its play? And there is no military action —from the nuclear confrontation in Cuba, October 1962, to the guerrilla warfare in South Viet Nam—which is not profoundly touched with politics and diplomacy at every point."

If a game historian or *rapporteur* is not assigned to the team, one player should assume this task at least to the ex-

[2] *The Dimensions of Diplomacy*, The Johns Hopkins Press, Baltimore, 1964, p. 53.

tent of keeping a check on pending events, as it is easy to forget that decisions do not always translate into immediate action, and that yesterday's decision may produce results that should be taken into account for tomorrow's play of the game. It may also be useful to keep a record of branch points—actions considered but discarded. A tape recorder can be helpful.

Teams having relatively minor parts in the game action can have fewer than five players. Two is a practical minimum, because one may start talking to himself. The United Nations, incidentally, is a frequent starter in a minor game role.

As a caveat for the inexperienced, it should be pointed out that the time available for the first team move will not permit much horsing around—best to get organized and on with the problem as rapidly as possible. In the normal case, time will be conserved by placing the specific crisis situation in the perspective of national (team) policy. National objectives should first be defined to fit the situation, after which appropriate strategies or courses of action to accomplish these objectives should be written out. Team strategies should include consideration of all likely contingencies. Thereafter it will be appropriate to consider the immediate decisions facing the team.

The team that is plainly the aggressor, in terms of the plot developed by the starting scenario, could very well be allowed time to study the situation before the full game actually begins, perhaps in consultation with Control, although this has not been a practice in the past. The Soviets obviously had a good deal more time to consider all aspects of a blockade of Berlin than did the Western allies, who suddenly found themselves confronted with a Soviet initiative in this connection. Incidentally, there is no reason why the good guys cannot be the ones to press the action: if you want to show your distaste for a policy of containment, for example, write yourself a plausible scenario rolling back the (iron) (bamboo) curtain.

Control has an evident need for players who can evaluate claims of the teams concerning their own and their antagonists' resources and capabilities, the capabilities of the United Nations under the game circumstances, the sublime and the ridiculous, and whatever. The Control team should assume the part of "Nature," playing the role of chance by introducing an occasional outside event to complicate the course of the game,[3] and must also simulate international actors other than those represented by the playing teams. The Control Chairman is well advised to require specialization of his staff, each of whom should keep a beady eye on at least one area of game interest and one of whom should maintain a careful score of events pending on the basis of past action. This function is similar to, but more important than, that suggested above for a team historian. It is the task of Control to keep the scenario moving along, which means that Control must never lose track of past team actions that should be reflected in Control's projections for future move periods. Here the blackboard becomes an invaluable aid, as abbreviated notations can be relied upon to jog someone's memory and can be erased when dealt with.

It is the task of Control to keep the scenario moving along. This means in the first instance that the Control team must develop, for distribution before each new team

---

[3] A flyer with an instrument rating must periodically undergo checks in a Link trainer. The outside operator can, and does, throw such curves as heavy turbulence or a sudden loss of altitude. The analogy with Control's role as "Nature" is obvious.

80

move during the exercise, an addition to the scenario posing the new situation resulting from team moves of the previous period. But Control must also adjudicate claims and complaints, make explanations, produce occasional intelligence (or garbled intelligence), introduce the inputs of Nature and non-assigned international actors, and—most importantly—so assess the interactions of team moves that the start of each new team period presents problems requiring brain-stretching decisions by all principal teams. The players on Control work harder than other gamers, and later at night. As one of its performers said on TV or, maybe, about TV, "Don't miss it, if you can."

Events extraneous to normal play should be introduced by Control with some purpose, such as to remind the teams that they operate in a world having interests other than those of the principal protagonists of the exercise. Control has to guard against going too far in introducing such events. One game in which I participated was thrown out of kilter by a sudden report (from Control) that the Soviets had shot down, over southern Europe, a ballistic missile which had been launched by Sweden for impact in the South Atlantic. The Blue team considered this occurrence of such significance to the existing "balance of terror" that it promptly abandoned the primary thread of the scenario in order to deal with what it considered a more serious crisis problem. Main strength and awkwardness were required to get matters back in train again.

Game procedures should be explained to all participants in a preliminary briefing session by the Game Director, who will previously have established them—although not necessarily beyond argument, if prior experience has a bearing.

Duration of the play is not fixed. Three days is suggested for a concentrated game: that is, a game which absorbs all the players' attention. Attenuated games, run on a part-time basis, can proceed for as long as two weeks without any considerable loss of interest. The concentrated game should begin with a Game Director's briefing which, in the Pentagon, is usually held a day or two before actual play commences, but which should be the first order of business at a sequestered location. The playing teams, in the normal concentrated game, move simultaneously and should be allowed several hours for each move. Assuming a morning briefing, the initial move period might take place from 1:00 to 5:00 P.M. (usually "1300 to 1700" in game practice). The Control team can then use the evening to project an addition to the scenario for distribution to the teams the next morning. This time, the teams should have perhaps three hours before turning in this paper work to Control by about noon. Control can then extend the scenario to permit the teams another move between, say, 3:00 and 6:00 P.M., after which Control takes over for the evening. On the third morning there can be a team period from 9:00 to 12:00, followed by a critique late in the afternoon or in the evening, after the participants in the exercise have had an opportunity to examine all game papers and to reassess their own actions.

This procedure, which obviously can be varied, permits a total of four team move periods, a practicable maximum for a three-day period. In many cases, three will prove enough to manage, especially if players have to make the 5:15 on the third day.

The Game Director will probably establish the requirement, previously suggested as a *desideratum,* that each team produce in writing a starting statement of its national objectives and related strategy (including contingency strategy) to fit the particular situation, and also provide Control with its initial decisions and actions. He will doubt-less suggest that the teams review objectives and strategies thus established, as the game progresses, in order to determine whether they are being consistent or whether, if inconsistent, they *should* have been consistent.

He should also suggest that various teams pursue either "normal," predictable strategies for the nations they represent, or "optimum" strategies without regard to what might be expected in view of past national patterns of action. This is the approach first instigated at RAND, when the "Soviet" players were told to play predictably and the "Americans" to attempt optimal strategies, with reportedly excellent results.

The Game Director ought to point out that "game time" can and probably will differ from real time. It will be up to the Control team to decide, on the basis of play as it develops, how the clock and the calendar are running. There will obviously be occasions when action is agonizingly concentrated, when the turn of events may hang on an answer over the "hot line" between Washington and Moscow. But there will also be occasions when a situation must mature; maybe Castro needs time to get enough Venezuelan guerrillas through his training schools before all hell can break loose in Caracas.

It also ought to be explained by the Game Director that security precautions must be maintained for game purposes, even where no actual classified information is being employed. "Game Classified" should be stamped on all papers developed during the game, other than those that are supposed to be open information; that is, available to all teams during the play. Team documents going to Control will almost invariably be "Game Classified" until move periods have been concluded, for they will not be intended for examination by hostile teams. Various announcements of events by Control, actions of international organizations, and reports in a game "newspaper," if there is one, are likely to be open information during the game.

The Game Director should explain that, while casual kibitzers are discouraged from wandering around the gaming area (a wise precaution), the teams may expect visits from members of the Control team. Such visits will be for the purpose of giving Control a leg up in starting its projection of the situation into the next round, and not for the purpose of providing the team with off-the-cuff decisions and interpretations. The Control Chairman may, for the same purpose, request oral reports from team chairmen after the teams have made their decisions but before resulting team documents have been prepared.

Finally, the Game Director should explain how communications will be handled.

Communications are of essential importance in crisis gaming. They should normally be in writing, unless the game is used to *test* other means of communication. Those that are not addressed to Control should nevertheless go through Control, which must be on top of everything transpiring in the game at all times. Action cannot normally be initiated by the teams *during* move periods, but is reserved for transmission to Control at the close of each period.

Papers originated during the game should be numbered sequentially, both for the game as a whole and for the originating agency. Thus, a question from the Red team to Control might be numbered 15 by the Red team, as being its 15th team document, and 37 by Control, as being the 37th document produced during the play of the game. The two numbers can appear in any agreed order on each paper, which also should carry an indication of the move period involved;

simple forms can easily be developed (see Chapter VII). For ready identification, communications are best produced on paper colored to identify their source. Ordinary white paper is useful for administrative purposes, light blue for the Blue team, pink for the Red team, white or buff for Control, yellow for another team, etc. Where tinted papers are hard to come by, the same effect can be achieved by marking with heavy colored crayon across the tops of papers. The game moves fast and benefits from every mechanical and optical aid available.

Although experimentation is always in order, it is emphasized again that best practice requires all communications to be in writing. This tends to keep the record straight and tends also to assure an even flow of information. A query addressed orally by Red to Control might produce oral information for Red only, in circumstances in which all teams should equally be entitled to the answer. But if the Red team sends to Control a written message: e.g., "Is the United Nations in session?"; it will be difficult for Control to avoid, through forgetfulness or carelessness, providing copies of the written reply to all teams.

Further on the business of oral communications, the temptation may arise to hold a conference among the contending teams, perhaps at the "summit" or, along moot court lines, as a rump session of the United Nations. Anything of this kind needs to be carefully reported in the first place, because the discussion is later almost certain to be interpreted differently by the participants, but the period required for acting out parts before even so impatiently uncritical an audience as the Game Director and the Control team will probably prove more than the allotted time can afford.

Written communications will provide ample difficulties of

interpretation. Oral ones can produce confusion resembling that in a story about the notoriously noisy London Underground. As one of its trains rumbled toward a station, one man leaned close to another and shouted, "I say, is this Wembley?" The other roared back, "No. It's Thursday." The first then replied in pitched tones, "So am I. Let's get off and get a drink."

Results in a game may not be equally felicitous.

Chapter VI
CUBA 1962 AS A GAME

It will be instructive to review the bidding in the Cuban missile crisis of 1962 as though the entire confrontation had been a game. Here again, nature and art are astonishingly close, suggesting that if an actual crisis can be reduced to game form, then a pretended crisis can come close to emulating a real one. A recapitulation of the Cuban crisis permits demonstration of the manner in which alternate game moves can be conducted to produce the "shoelace" pattern referred to in the preceding chapter. It also demonstrates one means of summarizing the results of an entire game.

In reconstructing Cuba 1962 as a game, I have relied on some, although not all, of the published reports, primarily those of the *New York Times,* but have not hesitated to invent gap-fillers where the record is lacking. The summary is therefore part fact and part fiction. If any of the latter should turn out to be fact, coincidence alone is responsible.

In a shoelace game, the periods for moves both by the teams and by Control can be varied to fit the requirements of the developing situation. Control can take advantage of this flexibility by allotting time on the basis of probable work to be done, provided of course that the participants in the exercise are fully available for purposes of the game. In the following summary, our imaginary Control is assumed to have used a flexible time schedule.

87

The Red and the Blue scenario summaries are displayed on facing pages, Red on the left, and so blocked out as to indicate what each was doing (or learning) during calendar periods roughly related to move periods. Because the initiative changes hands, one or the other of the protagonists will be seen to be active while the other is passive during most of the game intervals, to the extent in fact of producing a few blank pages.

Move Period
0800–1200, First Day

RED INITIATIVE

In May 1962 the Cuban situation reached a point calling for some measure of real and open Soviet military support. Castro, whose impulse in openly declaring himself a Marxist and his country a Soviet affiliate had seriously compromised Cuban (and Communist) ability to penetrate elsewhere in Latin America, was convinced to the point of hysteria that American invasion was imminent. Whether this could in fact be regarded as likely, the prevailing Havana mood required that Soviet support of Castro be publicly displayed in Cuba.

At a series of June meetings in Moscow, Castro's representatives demanded immediate large shipments of sophisticated arms and equipment, and also the provision of both defensive and offensive nuclear weapon systems. They professed Castro's conviction that a credible threat of nuclear destruction would alone deter the U.S. from invading, and also that such a threat could best be made credible if Cuba itself possessed the means of nuclear attack.

While the Cuban economy was becoming wholly dependent upon bloc support, and Cuba was thus in a poor trading position, it was nevertheless apparent that a jittery Castro might be capable, if rebuffed, of a rupture in political ties that would represent a sharp blow to Soviet prestige and would entail the loss of Cuban potentialities for the advancement of world socialism.

(Decisions made, marking the end of the first Red team move, follow hereafter.)

BLUE

Move Period
0800—1200, First Day

In the summer of 1962 it became apparent that Castro, having placed Cuba in the position of a semi-satellite within the Communist bloc, was beginning to receive extensive Soviet aid, including military aid.

Soviet arms shipments flowed increasingly thereafter into Cuba. In September the President responded to widely expressed concern by announcing that the military build-up in Cuba appeared a defensive one not warranting U.S. intervention. "Were it to be otherwise," he said, "the gravest issues would arise."

The Kremlin problem was to satisfy Castro and at the same time to strengthen the Soviet power position, but without pressing matters to the point where a flat showdown with the U.S. might become necessary.

It was out of the question that Castro should be provided nuclear weapons, none of which had yet been made available to any Soviet allies. However, Marshal Malinovsky offered to the Politburo a suggestion that was subsequently acted upon. This was the bold proposal that MRBMs/IRBMs be installed clandestinely on Cuban soil in Soviet hands, protected by surface-to-air missiles (SAMs), some of which might be manned by Cubans. The proposition offered several points of advantage, aside from at least partial satisfaction of Castro's demands. It would, if successfully accomplished, produce a dramatic shift in the relative strategic strike threat situation. It would enhance Soviet ability to apply pressure at sensitive spots—particularly Berlin. And it would create a Soviet overseas base that might prove a most valuable bargaining counter in possible subsequent roll-back negotiations. The danger of a bold U.S. reaction during the Soviet build-up was discounted by the Politburo on the basis of an anticipated U.S. tendency to temporize and compromise.

Consultation with Castro resulted in his acceptance that Soviet offensive missiles should be installed on Cuban soil, provided missile air defenses, late-model interceptor fighters, late-model tanks, and effective coastal defense weapons were generously supplied to Cuban forces. The bargain was concluded on this basis, with maximum security precautions.

☐ BLUE ☐

⸻ RED ⸻

The program previously decided upon was placed on a crash basis to provide for a virtual prefabrication in the U.S.S.R. of missile sites for shipment, with missiles, in a number of cargo vessels that required immediate modification for the purpose. Soviet experts at once departed for Cuba in order to select sites, etc. By mid-October virtually all the men and equipment were on hand in Cuba, and the work was well forward toward a planned completion date of early December. Nuclear warheads, afloat in submarines, would be available to complete the Soviet coup on or shortly after that date.

BLUE

(Control Works 1100–1400, First Day)
Move Period
1400–1730, First Day

BLUE INITIATIVE

By early October, U.S. intelligence had accumulated numerous reports (some from Cuban refugees) that Soviet military equipment in Cuba included missiles of considerable size. The intelligence presumption remained that any Soviet missiles deployed to Cuba would necessarily be defensive in type, particularly as it was considered most unlikely that the Soviet Union would permit any deployment of its nuclear warheads to a location as remote and vulnerable as Cuba. Nevertheless, photo reconnaissance was expanded to cover all Cuban territory.

This reconnaissance produced photographic proof, the first of which dated from October 14, that the Soviets were actually emplacing long-range offensive missiles (MRBMs/IRBMs) in Cuba, and that several sites were within days of attaining operational status. A total of some forty MRBMs/IRBMs were detected in exposed positions. In addition, a similar number of Soviet IL 28 (Beagle) light bombers were photographed under assembly and in crates on Cuban airfields. It was evident also that, whether or not Soviet missiles in Cuba were ever to possess nuclear warheads, the United States could act only on the assumption that they would in fact do so.

The initial photo intelligence resulted in a series of conferences of the President and his principal advisers. On October 18, Soviet Ambassador Gromyko, summoned to the White House, repeated prior Soviet assurances that

95

arms shipments to Cuba from the Soviet Union were wholly defensive. But U.S. intelligence had hardened on the offensive nature of the missiles in Cuba, and the President held an intensive series of conferences with his political and military advisers during the weekend of October 20–21. By the afternoon of Monday, October 22, a number of decisions had been reached.

(These decisions, marking the end of the first Blue team move, are reflected in the following passage of this scenario.)

Action to forestall operational status for the Soviet offensive missiles in Cuba was plainly imperative. Three schools of thought emerged within the tight group of presidential advisers. Some felt that immediate military action in the form of air attack or airborne and amphibious invasion, or both, should be undertaken. A minority view held that a trade should first be offered to Chairman Khrushchev, perhaps of U.S. missile bases in Turkey and Italy in exchange for the Soviet Cuban base, in view of the real possibility that military action might lead to general war. A third view, which came to be shared by the President, was that an immediate sea blockade of Cuba should be imposed to initiate a period during which the Soviets might be persuaded to withdraw their missiles from Cuba under threat of even more positive military action by the United States. Should this effort fail, direct military action would then be necessary.

The President's decision was to impose a naval blockade (to be described as a "quarantine," for the purpose of avoiding harsh words) on any movement of offensive weapons to Cuba, while also initiating a prompt build-up of forces in

RED

BLUE

Florida for an invasion that might become necessary. At the same time, U.S. forces everywhere were to be alerted and the SAC airborne alert materially stepped up. A virtual ultimatum would be handed to Khrushchev.

RED

(Control Works 1630–2100, First Day)
Move Period
0830–1200, Second Day

RED INITIATIVE

During the first half of October, a sharp increase in U.S. overflights of Cuba occurred. Inasmuch as Soviet SAMs were not yet operational, no effective counteraction could be taken. The American press also began publicizing reports of Cuban refugees that offensive missiles were being emplaced in Cuba.

Missile technicians in Cuba were instructed to redouble their efforts, already proceeding day and night, after Gromyko reported that Kennedy, on October 18, had called him in to ask whether Soviet missiles were being emplaced in Cuba (denied by Gromyko).

Over the weekend of October 20–21, the Soviet Embassy in Washington reported a spate of rumors concerning a crisis situation, thought to center on Cuba. It was evident that time might be running out for the attempt to emplace missiles in Cuba on a clandestine basis.

At seven on the evening of October 22, Washington time, President Kennedy made a nation-wide TV address in which he announced discovery of the missile effort in Cuba. At the same time, the President announced a naval blockade of offensive weapons into Cuba, to be effective at 10:00 A.M., October 24 (Washington time), and not to be lifted until the Soviet missile sites in Cuba had been dismantled and withdrawn. He proclaimed that the firing of a missile from Cuba against any target in the Western Hemisphere would be treated as an attack on the United States.

100

BLUE

Public rumors of an impending crisis, suspected to involve Cuba, had been building in the United States for several days, although the actual situation had been prevented from leaking through extraordinary security precautions. Announcement was made the afternoon of October 22 that the President would address the nation on television that same evening on a matter of "national urgency." Dean Acheson, as a Presidential emissary, was then already on his way to Paris with advance information for NATO allies.

In his address, the President announced the existence of Soviet offensive missiles in Cuba; proclaimed the naval "quarantine" to become effective at 10:00 A.M., October 24; demanded the "prompt dismantling and withdrawal" of the Soviet missile bases; and made clear that a missile attack from Cuba against any target in the Western Hemisphere would be regarded as an attack on the United States.

The issue was thus placed squarely up to the Soviet Union —not to Cuba—on a global basis.

RED

Coincident with its delivery by the President, a copy of this address was handed to the Soviet Ambassador in Washington, and arrived at the Kremlin to precipitate an emergency meeting of the Politburo at 5:00 A.M., Moscow time.

By the time that the Politburo was assembled, reports had filtered in to indicate that SAC was mounting a maximum airborne alert and that a marked movement of U.S. forces was occurring into and within Florida. Within the Politburo there was a sense of shock at the speed and abruptness with which the United States had acted to avert a threat that had not yet materialized. Several members could not bring themselves to believe that the Soviet estimate of probable U.S. reaction was so far from the mark, and considered Kennedy's actions must amount to bluff.

But a clear test of U.S. intentions would emerge from the conduct of the American blockade of Cuba, toward which a convoy of Soviet cargo vessels was headed in mid-Atlantic. If the United States stopped and boarded these vessels, temporization would be indicated.

(Decisions made follow hereafter.)

It was decided that the convoy should be instructed to proceed, but that the twelve vessels carrying "offensive" weapons should leave the convoy and avoid the blockade. A Soviet tanker—obviously not carrying weapons—would penetrate the blockade first. This would be followed—on a "fail-safe" basis—by a Lebanese vessel under Soviet charter, boarding of which by the U.S. Navy would not set the precedent that a Soviet vessel manned by Soviet citizens had been so molested. At the same time, Soviet and Warsaw Pact forces would be alerted and protests against U.S. "piracy" pressed in the UN and elsewhere.

It was also decided that Bertrand Russell should be privately urged to appeal to Chairman Khrushchev for a "peacemaking" effort.

BLUE

RED

(Control Works 1100—1300, Second Day)
Move Period
1300—1400, Second Day

Action was set in train along the lines previously decided upon.

BLUE

BLUE INITIATIVE

Moscow's initial response to the President's speech—delayed several hours—was a Tass statement bitterly condemning the blockade as "piracy," and an alerting of Soviet and Warsaw Pact forces.

In Washington, immediate unanimous approval of the Organization of American States was given to a resolution to oppose, with force if necessary, the emplacement of Soviet offensive missiles in Cuba. Within the United Nations, Ambassador Stevenson demanded withdrawal of the missile bases. Soviet Ambassador Zorin called for an end to the blockade and suggested negotiation to "remove the threat of war."

At sea, the resolution of the United States was evidently to be tested shortly. Air reconnaissance determined during October 21 and 22 that a convoy of Soviet vessels carrying jet aircraft, etc., toward Cuba had altered course with the evident intention of avoiding the naval quarantine. However, one Soviet tanker remained on course for Havana, and bloc vessels of other registries were also proceeding into the blockade.

(Decisions made follow hereafter.)

At a short, tense meeting with his selected advisers, Kennedy decided that instructions to the Navy should provide for temporizing with the Soviets as long as possible, in that the Soviet vessel should be halted but not boarded. Other bloc vessels would be halted and searched.

105

Move Period
1400–1700, Second Day

RED INITIATIVE

As of Thursday, October 25, in Moscow, it was fully apparent to the Politburo that the United States meant business. A Soviet vessel had been stopped at sea and a charter vessel boarded and inspected. While Washington was displaying reasonable forbearance in certain respects—polite acceptance of overtures for negotiation from Chairman Khrushchev as well as U Thant, and abstinence from direct attack on Cuba—there was every indication that Kennedy would take action to demolish or remove the missile sites unless this was first promised by the Soviet Union.

(Decisions and actions follow.)

It was decided that an offer should be drawn up to trade U.S. missile sites in Turkey for Soviet missile sites in Cuba, as had already been suggested in the American press by Walter Lippmann, although without indication of U.S. governmental interest in the proposal.

During the evening of October 25, Khrushchev took it upon himself to compose an earnest plea to Kennedy for cooperation toward peace, on terms that implicitly provided for removal of Soviet missile sites in exchange for an American promise not to invade Cuba. The Chairman reported his action at a Politburo meeting the following morning. He was persuaded to endorse a second message, firmer in tone and adding the proposal for a trade in missile sites. However, unknown to the Politburo, Khrushchev had already acted through intelligence channels to propose a settlement along the lines proposed in his initial letter.

BLUE

Within the United Nations a bitter debate continued between Stevenson and Zorin, with the latter denying the existence of offensive weapons in Cuba, even in the face of photographic evidence which he described as "falsified." Secretary General U Thant urged both sides to avoid incidents at sea. The Soviets agreed to keep Soviet vessels away from the quarantine area and the United States promised to avoid direct confrontation for "the next few days." But U Thant was informed that the United States was immovably insistent on removal of the missile sites from Cuba.

Within Cuba, U.S. air coverage indicated that work was continuing on the missile sites and also that camouflage measures were being introduced.

[   ]RED[   ]

Both Khrushchev's own first message and the Politburo-directed sequel were transmitted to the United States. In addition, the intelligence chief in the Soviet Washington Embassy approached an American media representative as a go-between with the White House in connection with the Chairman's private intelligence initiative.

BLUE ☐

BLUE INITIATIVE

The State Department message center on Friday evening, October 25, began to receive a long and conciliatory message from Khrushchev. The tone was one of urgency in averting the possibility of a nuclear war. Suggested—although not explicitly—was a withdrawal of offensive weapons from Cuba, under UN supervision, in exchange for a U.S. guarantee against the invasion of Cuba. While the President's advisers were drafting a reply on Saturday morning, a second Khrushchev letter arrived, offering to trade Soviet bases in Cuba for the U.S. NATO missile base in Turkey.

A brief White House statement was issued, indicating that work must stop on the Cuban sites before sensible negotiations could be undertaken.

On Saturday afternoon a report was received that Cuba had shot down one U.S. reconnaissance aircraft—possibly two—and that Castro was on TV proclaiming total defiance of the U.S. Was this unilateral action or was Moscow involved?

(Decisions and actions follow.)

It was decided that there should be an immediate call-up of 14,000 air reservists to make it clear that counteraction would be taken should air reconnaissance of Cuba be further interfered with.

The first, still secret, Khrushchev letter had, in effect, admitted the existence of Soviet offensive weapons in Cuba

109

RED

and remained to be answered—or ignored. At the same time, anti-aircraft rocket firing had occurred in Cuba, making it doubtful that the situation could remain under control much longer. It was decided that the President would reply at once to the secret Khrushchev letter, making no reference to the second letter or to Turkish bases, but accepting the proposal—if such a proposal had been intended—of a Soviet withdrawal of offensive weapons under UN supervision in exchange for assurances against the invasion of Cuba.

⬛RED⬜

RED INITIATIVE

While awaiting a response to the two most recent letters from Chairman Khrushchev to President Kennedy, the Politburo received a violent and critical message from Castro, demanding Soviet action to lift the U.S. blockade and affirming Cuba's intent to halt violations of its sovereignty by American overflights. At almost the same time, the Soviet Mission in Havana reported that the Cubans had, in fact, brought down at least one U.S. aircraft. A message was sent to the Chief of Soviet Mission in Havana, instructing him to hold Castro in check by all means possible, to include the threat of severance of Soviet aid and the promise that Cuba would be protected against invasion.

Early Saturday, October 27, a Kennedy letter was received, responding to the Chairman's personal letter and accepting its implicit offer while making no mention of the Turkish missile base.

(Decisions follow.)

Despite the existence of strong support for a "harder" line within the Politburo (but not within the Soviet military leadership), decision was made to liquidate the crisis on this basis. A letter was drawn up in which Chairman Khrushchev promised an immediate halt of work on the missile sites (all MRBMs, but not the IRBMs, actually became operational coincident with this move), and recrating and return of the missiles to the Soviet Union with UN representatives to "verify the dismantling." He, on his part, would accept President Kennedy's assurance that there would be no invasion of Cuba.

112

BLUE

⌐RED⌐

After preliminary notice of an important announcement, this letter was made public by the Moscow radio at such time as to become known in Washington the morning of Sunday, October 28.

Mikoyan was ordered to Havana for negotiations with Castro which—quite evidently—would be likely to produce awkward and painful moments. The propaganda apparatus was instructed to play up the sacrifices of the Soviet Union in accepting U.S. encirclement and even sea blockade while itself withdrawing even the slightest appearance of provocation—all to avoid nuclear war that could only imperil all peoples, etc.

Critique Period
1500—1800, Third Day

BLUE

(Control Works 1000–1200, Third Day)
Move Period
1300–1500, Third Day

BLUE ACTION

President Kennedy's letter to Chairman Khrushchev was made public and also delivered to the Soviet Embassy in Washington at 7:00 P.M., October 27, Washington time.

At almost the same time, President Kennedy remarked to his chief advisers that matters werc now at a point where the situation could go "either way."

In the meantime, however, on October 26, an extraordinary approach for a settlement reached the White House through John A. Scali of the American Broadcasting Company. Scali had received, from A. S. Fomin of the Soviet Embassy in Washington, a proposal purporting to emanate from Khrushchev that offered Soviet withdrawal of missiles from Cuba in exchange for a U.S. promise not to invade Cuba. Authenticity of the proposal appeared possible, if questionable.

Critique Period
1500–1800, Third Day

If we were actually running a critique of the Cuba confrontation of 1962, along game lines, we would be compelled to point out that the starting scenario is too fantastic for serious consideration. Imagine the United States clandestinely supporting an outlaw movement to overthrow a Batista dictatorship in Cuba, only to see the new regime rapidly attach Cuba to Moscow, and then to discover the latter secretly emplacing missiles in Cuba with which to threaten the United States!

But the Cuba confrontation was a sober fact of the long, cold war, and when it came to an end it could be recognized as a massive landmark in relations between the Soviet Union and the United States. Thenceforth, for a long time—perhaps for a very long time—there could hardly be further Soviet tests of American will and determination at levels invoking any real prospect of thermonuclear warfare. A whole new cycle in international relations was introduced.

One would be hard put to develop valid criticism of the manner in which the Washington participants handled this crisis. Considering the embarrassment of their position, the Moscow participants must also be given high marks for the skill with which they disengaged.

Chapter VII

KASHMIR 1966 AS A FICTIONAL CRISIS

The all-too-genuine Cuban crisis of 1962 can, as we have seen, be described in game format. To provide further graphic demonstration for this book, I directed, early in February 1965, the play of a pretended crisis centering on Kashmir in late 1966. My hope is that readers will find it has the flavor of an actual crisis.

Presented here is a compressed and somewhat edited version of the documents developed for and in this exercise, enough perhaps to illustrate the "simultaneous move" technique and to provide an explanation of developments during the play. My own occasional comments are offered in italics. However, before exposing the record, a few preliminary remarks seem indicated.

1. A special artificiality is introduced into the play because of the requirement that one team represent both the United States and India, and another team both Communist China and Pakistan. India and Pakistan can of course be expected, game or no game, to have purposes and policies at variance with those of their friends and allies. In order to develop the plot, it was necessary to involve too many countries for convenient representation by separate teams. As a means of partial correction, Control was asked to introduce, when appropriate, distinct Indian and Pakistani ploys.

2. A "fact book" of background materials was made

available prior to the play. This included several chapters from *Communist China in World Politics* by a colleague, Harold C. Hinton,[1] selected articles from *Foreign Affairs,* information from *The Military Balance 1964–65,*[2] largely fictitious projections of various military postures in and around South Asia, and, of course, a map of the area involved.

3. Printing costs prevent distinguishing among team documents through the use of tinted paper, as was done in the game itself. The message form accomplishes this for present purposes.

4. I do not really think that Pakistan will behave as badly as I picture her doing in the starting scenario, nor do I really expect Communist China to give Pakistan, or any country, the kind of blank-check backing I have her providing.

5. Irrelevancies, repetitions, slips, and minor errors of fact are detectable in the record, which I have not attempted to "purify." They occurred in this game as they are likely to occur in any game.

Now, the Kashmir crisis of 1966.

Starting Scenario

The Indian subcontinent after the British departed was politically symbolic of the state in which they found it; that is, divided. Instead of numerous principalities, however, there were two sovereign states. Unity of the subcontinent had proven unattainable, essentially because the dominant Hindu element was unable or unwilling to assure

---

[1] For publication in late 1965 or early 1966 by Houghton Mifflin Company, Boston.

[2] The Institute for Strategic Studies, 18 Adam St., London, W.C. 2, 1964.

that concentrated Moslem groups would retain minority rights. Even with the acceptance of division, India numbered in its huge population about half as many Moslems —perhaps 45,000,000—as in all Pakistan, which itself was divided, a thousand miles of semi-hostile India separating East and West Pakistan.

Celebrations of sovereignty for both India and Pakistan were marred by the massacre of Moslems within India and of Hindus and Sikhs within Pakistan, poisoning mutual relations at the outset. But, in addition, the Congress Party of India made no effort to disguise its conviction that Pakistan could not prove viable and must eventually rejoin India on Indian terms. This the Pakistani were determined to avoid, and their determination was translated with time into an obsession with the military threat they considered India to pose against their security. It was this, rather than what they regarded as the lesser threat from the Soviet Union, that impelled Pakistan to enter a Southeast Asia Treaty Organization which the United States conceived as directed against Communism. By 1961, in fact, the United States had agreed that Pakistan could unequivocally use U.S. military aid to maintain its security.

Well before 1961, armed conflict had occurred between India and Pakistan over Kashmir, which, despite its predominantly Moslem population, the government of India insisted upon possessing. A fragile UN cease-fire was imposed with difficulty.

"Non-aligned" India was regarded by the United States until the late fifties as unreliable and even immoral, the notion being that India ought to stand up and be counted alongside other democracies and the West. Both the Soviets and the Communist Chinese maintained generally good relations with India throughout the same period, the former recognizing the Indian claim to Kashmir and initiating a number of Indian aid programs, and the latter from time to time promulgating the agreeable myth of 2000 years of Sino-Indian friendship. In fact, the Communist Chinese nurtured territorial claims in the Himalayan region that could only be resisted by the Indians. These claims, in an area where boundaries had always been amorphous, included territory in the region from Nepal north to Sinkiang, China, including what India considered to be a part of Kashmir, and, in the east, the old North East Frontier Agency north of Indian Assam. The Chinese intent, as would shortly become clear, was to control the principal Himalayan passes through possession of the southern slopes and to protect military roads which the Chinese began to build in secrecy in the disputed areas as early as the late fifties.

In 1962 Communist China, which had gradually been developing accords with a Pakistan dissatisfied with the extent of U.S. military aid, concluded with Pakistan an agreement delimiting their common border in the area of Kashmir west of the cease-fire line. This followed a similar agreement between Communist China and Burma. India, the Chinese let it be known, was recalcitrant in approaching a reasonable border settlement. In 1958 the Indians had learned that Chinese forces were present in disputed Himalayan border areas. In 1961 they began probes of their own, with a misplaced faith in the military preparations for which Defense Minister Krishna Menon had been responsible. By early fall, surprisingly numerous Chinese forces had driven the Indians back both in Ladakh and in the North East Frontier Agency and were threatening the Assam plain.

The prospect of further fighting ended for the time being when the Communist Chinese forces were suddenly pulled back, although continuing to remain forward in the western sector of any line to which India could willingly agree.

During this humiliating experience, which exposed the extent of Indian military weakness, India called upon the United States for aid in the form of combat equipment, especially anti-aircraft weapons and fighter aircraft. The United States responded positively, attempting to adjust its aid so that the Indian-Pakistani balance would be unaffected. However, Pakistan became disillusioned and even enraged that a neutral India should now reap rewards as great as, or greater than, any an allied Pakistan had received from the United States. There were threats of Pakistani withdrawal from SEATO and from other forms of collaboration with the United States.

The weakened influence of India in world affairs, resulting from its painful brush with Communist China and from the death of Prime Minister Nehru, led the Soviet Union to begin a diplomatic advance toward Pakistan that by the summer of 1965 was challenging the strong Communist Chinese position there and was also leading Pakistan to show increasing intransigeance in its relations with the United States. Aid from the competing major Communist powers evidently looked to President Ayub Khan like a potentially satisfactory replacement for American aid, economic and military.

Prime Minister Shastri, Nehru's successor, was faced with separatist inclinations on the part of several important Indian states, exacerbated by the attempt to impose Hindi as the official language throughout India; a major challenge to his Congress Party from the Hindu nationalist Jan Sangh; and the promise of treachery and subversion from the "leftist" Communist Party which favored Communist China in the ideological quarrel splitting the Communist world.

121

The potentially equal threat from the Moscow-oriented Communist "right" could be, and was, ignored for the time being because of currently friendly Soviet policy toward India.

The Jan Sangh, by the summer of 1965, aided thus by activities of the Communist left, had persuaded elements even in the Congress Party to support a program of enhanced military preparedness, to include the eventual development of nuclear weaponry, and to insist upon an early "restoration" of the northern frontier.

Possessing plain evidence of their revolutionary intent, the Indian Government acted on December 30, 1964, with decisive surprise, to round up and imprison some 800 leaders of the Communist left. Home Minister Nanda stated the reason: ". . . there is now a Communist power across the Indian border which makes revolutionary activities within this country far more opportune. The object of the party is to promote internal revolution to synchronize with a fresh Chinese attack." The government also released a secret circular of the Communist left that described the Chinese Communists as "liberators" and further said that "the activities on the northern borders of the country were an extension of the revolutionary struggle in the southern part of the country." Kashmir, Kerala, the North East Frontier Agency, and Nagaland were described as the "weakest links" in the defenses of India. The circular promised that if they could be brought under control the whole of India would be brought under Communism.

In September 1965, as the result of the threat from the Communist left and the nationalistic pressure of the Jan Sangh, Prime Minister Shastri was led to order a cautious probing advance of Indian forces into the "no man's land" then separating them from the Chinese outposts. The Indian move was met by a brusque Chinese response that had the result, after a series of minor engagements, of driving the Indian forces back to their former positions. The advent of winter cold therefore saw the military situation little changed from what it had previously been. Indian intelligence was clear, however, on the point that the Chinese had been reinforcing their Himalayan forces while building up local stocks of military supplies and ammunition.

During the winter of 1965–66 the Peking Government maintained a constant and virulent attack upon the Indian Government and its actions of "invading" Communist China and of imprisoning Communist Party members. Peking promised that the masses of India would soon be "liberated" from an oppressive "reactionary nationalist" government. In January 1966 there occurred within India, at the several points where leftist Communist prisoners were being held, an impressive demonstration of the power of the Communist left to plan and to act. Simultaneous and massive jail breaks took place, resulting in the clean escape of all but about forty of the detainees. Assiduous pursuit and a continuing search discovered none of the escapees as the year wore on, although by April a series of "manifestos," calling for revolution in India, began to emanate from Peking in the name of former Communist officials of the state of Kerala.

The military flare-up along the Sino-Indian border in the fall of 1965, while producing a stony silence from Moscow, which was maintaining excellent relations with both India and Pakistan, had evoked anxious concern from the United States, as well as from Commonwealth nations, including of course the United Kingdom. The latter offered to mediate the disagreement, but received no reply from Communist China and little encouragement from India, which was beginning to believe that nothing savoring of moderation would satisfy Peking.

In March 1966 a Hindu fanatic was beaten to death in Lahore by a mob convinced that he had "defiled" a mosque. Within hours, at Amritsar across the border in India, a Hindu mob similarly murdered a Moslem. There followed a flare-up of violence in both India and Pakistan, brought under control after ten terrible days in which several hundred Moslems and nearly as many Hindus and Sikhs were killed. The governments of the two countries began at that time to trade accusations as to degrees of official connivance in the religious massacres, leading by early summer to a situation of near hostility between the two countries. Shots were exchanged from time to time in Kashmir.

As the summer of 1966 began, the course of world events other than in the Asiatic area continued to flow much as it had since 1964. The struggle in Southeast Asia persisted, as threats to the northern and eastern Thai borders brought a sharp increase in U.S. military aid to Thailand and the increasing use of the Bangkok area as an American support center: U.S.-Thai cooperation reached a high point. Four Polaris submarines had been attached to the U.S. 7th Fleet in the Pacific. A carrier task force of the U.S. Navy had been deployed in the Indian Ocean. Indonesia was locked with Malaysia in a hit-and-run war of feints and raids, in which all British, Australian, and New Zealand forces available for the area, except bomber forces, were defensively engaged. The United Nations was in session, the Soviet Union a member in good standing as the result of a "formula" solution to the delinquencies in its support payments.

"Game classified" addenda to this scenario, as follow, were made available to the indicated teams at the outset of the first move period.

GAME CLASSIFIED

Blue (U.S.-Indian) Addendum to Starting Scenario

Early in August 1966, India publicly announced its discovery of active, "offensive" Communist Chinese military preparations in the Himalayas north of Sikkim. Shortly thereafter a U.S. reconnaissance aircraft brought back photographic confirmation of increased Chinese military activity in the area. The United States, as well as the United Kingdom, answered an Indian appeal for additional arms aid by sending a military mission to New Delhi. Even before the mission arrived, on August 20, Chinese nationalist intelligence, confirmed by U.S. reconnaissance, began reporting intensified military activity in Fukien province opposite Taiwan, including the arrival of several army divisions from the north and several additional squadrons of MIG fighters.

Pakistan was prompt in denouncing the Indian call for additional American arms aid and in protesting to Washington any possibility of favorable consideration. Public announcement that the United States was sending a new military mission to India resulted in a private warning, conveyed by President Ayub Khan to the American Ambassador in Rawalpindi, that India was in fact building toward an attack on Pakistan and that, if the United States showed even a cursory interest in improving Indian capabilities to such an end, Pakistan would have no choice but to regard U.S. policy as hostile to its interest. The American reply was prompt in stating that any military aid extended by the United States to India would be for the sole purpose of improving Indian defenses against Communist Chinese border threats.

125

On August 25 the government of Pakistan announced Pakistan's immediate withdrawal from membership in SEATO and from the 1959 Bilateral Agreement with the United States. At the same time, Lahore began a series of bitter complaints respecting "aggressive Indian incursions" across the cease-fire line in Kashmir. Secretary General U Thant was unable to confirm such incursions through truce teams of the United Nations in the area, and in fact on August 30 all communication with truce teams on the Pakistani side of the cease-fire line came to an end.

Prior to mid-day in New York on August 31, reports were received from truce teams with Indian forces in Kashmir to the effect that Pakistan had in fact launched an attack from which Indian forces were recoiling. This was confirmed by early news service reports and was followed almost immediately in Washington by an official Indian notification that Pakistan was attempting a military take-over of all of Kashmir. The Indian Ambassador also reported that Chinese forces appeared to be moving to extend their occupation of the Aksai Chin, regarded by India as a part of Kashmir.

The day drew to a close amid reports of panic and rioting in India, particularly in West Bengal, where there were also reports of extensive mob violence against Moslem inhabitants.

It is now September 1, 1966.

The Blue (U.S.-Indian) team is requested to prepare statements of the objectives of both countries in the present situation, to list various contingent courses of action that will be taken to meet estimated turns in the situation, and to state the specific immediate actions to be taken by the two countries, jointly or separately.

GAME CLASSIFIED

Yellow (Sino-Pakistani) Addendum to Starting Scenario

The 1962 Sino-Pakistani border agreement contained a secret protocol, the terms of which provided for Pakistani recognition of the Chinese claim to territory that India regarded as a part of Kashmir in return for assurance by Communist China that she would "concretely" support Pakistan's claims to Kashmir "at an appropriate time."

Peking, in the late winter of 1966, informed Pakistan of its intention "to eject interlopers from the south of China," commencing with favorable summer weather, and suggested that the consequent probable diversion of Indian military forces should offer a favorable opportunity for Pakistan to assume its "rightful control" over Kashmir. Pakistan responded by expressing concern over the position of East Pakistan, vulnerable as it was to a surrounding India and to internal Hindu subversions, should Pakistan make any offensive move in the Kashmir area. Peking, with unconcealed contempt for Indian military capabilities, assured Lahore that Chinese forces would be so poised as to counter Indian threats to East Pakistan. Agreement on mutual support for military operations to achieve Pakistani occupation of Kashmir and Chinese occupation of all Himalayan border claims was thereafter reached, the target date being September 1, 1966.

In early August, India announced the discovery of "offensive" Himalayan military preparations by Communist Chinese forces and called on the United States, the Soviet Union, and the United Kingdom for additional arms aid. The United States and the United Kingdom responded at once by sending military missions to New Delhi, American alarm being enhanced by what the U.S. press described as a "military build-up" in Fukien province opposite Taiwan. This was a precautionary build-up on the part of Peking, looking to the prospect of military action in the south. Pakistan, on August 25, after protesting the extension of further military aid to India, especially from the United States, renounced both its membership in SEATO and the 1959 Bilateral Agreement with the United States. At the same time, Pakistan commenced a series of complaints respecting "aggressive Indian incursions" across the cease-fire line in Kashmir. UN truce teams in the area were unable to confirm such Indian incursions. On August 30 all communications from truce teams on the Pakistani side of the cease-fire line broke off (the teams having been taken into protective custody by the Pakistani Army). Early on August 31, Pakistani forces, which had been moving up nocturnally for the purpose, crossed the cease-fire line in Kashmir. Indian troops were driven back, truce teams on their side of the cease-fire line moving with them and reporting back to the United Nations firm evidence of a Pakistani violation of the truce.

The Chinese moved simultaneously, in exceptionally favorable weather conditions, to complete the military occupation of all Himalayan border areas claimed by them. A relatively heavy movement of Chinese forces also shortly became evident toward and within Sikkim north of Thanggu, as waves of alarm, rioting, and threats to Moslem citizens took place within India. In West Bengal, by the close of day on August 31, more than 200 Moslems had met death at the hands of mobs.

It is now September 1, 1966.

The Yellow (Sino-Pakistani) team is requested to prepare statements of the objectives of both countries in the present

128

situation, to list various contingent courses of action that will be adopted to meet different responses to actions already taken, and to state the specific further actions the two countries take at this time, jointly or separately.

GAME CLASSIFIED

Red (Soviet) Addendum to Starting Scenario

The Soviets realized with some surprise, as the summer of 1966 advanced, that the Peking press had for some months soft-pedaled its previously harsh criticism of the Soviet leadership. Late in July Peking newspapers began emphasizing the theme of "socialist solidarity" and by mid-August occasional reminders appeared that Communist China and the Soviet Union, regardless of past family squabbles, were in the final analysis staunch military allies bound to support each other against aggression from any source. Eyebrows began to rise in Moscow.

They stopped rising as Indian reports of Chinese military activity in the Himalayan region multiplied, reports the Soviets soon discovered through their own intelligence to have a strong basis in fact. A public Indian demand on the United States for increased arms aid was paralleled by a private Indian diplomatic approach requesting Soviet military aid. Moscow reserved its reply, while the United States and the United Kingdom each sent military teams to New Delhi for obvious exploratory purposes.

Pakistan, in evident protest that the United States should consider providing further military aid to India, suddenly made public on August 25 its immediate withdrawal from SEATO and at the same time renounced its 1959 Bilateral Agreement with the United States. Pakistan simultaneously began a series of shrill complaints concerning what were alleged as "aggressive Indian incursions" across the cease-fire line in Kashmir. Reports from UN headquarters in New York indicated no confirmation of Indian truce violations from UN truce teams on the ground in Kashmir. On August 30 the UN Secretary General informed the Security Council that all communication with truce teams on the Pakistani side of the cease-fire line had suddenly ceased.

In Moscow late on August 31 reports began to arrive that fighting had broken out in Kashmir. Confirmation came almost at once in a communication from the Indian Ambassador in Moscow and in a dispatch from UN headquarters in New York. Pakistan was reported to have crossed the cease-fire line and to be in the process of driving Indian troops out of Kashmir, aided possibly by what was reported as a Communist Chinese foray into that part of the Aksai Chin, Kashmir, which they were not already occupying. As the day drew to a close, Moscow received reports of extensive Indian rioting and panic, especially in West Bengal, where mob violence had already resulted in the death of some 200 Moslem inhabitants.

It is now September 1, 1966.

The Red (Soviet) team is requested to prepare a statement of its objectives in the present situation, to list various contingent courses of action the Soviet Union will take to meet estimated possible turns in the situation, and to state specific immediate actions to be taken by the Soviet Union.

YELLOW NO. 1   GAME PAPER NO. 1
YELLOW TO CONTROL   MOVE PERIOD NO. 1

Clarification is requested as to the degree of escalation permitted within the rules of the game.

FIGURE 4

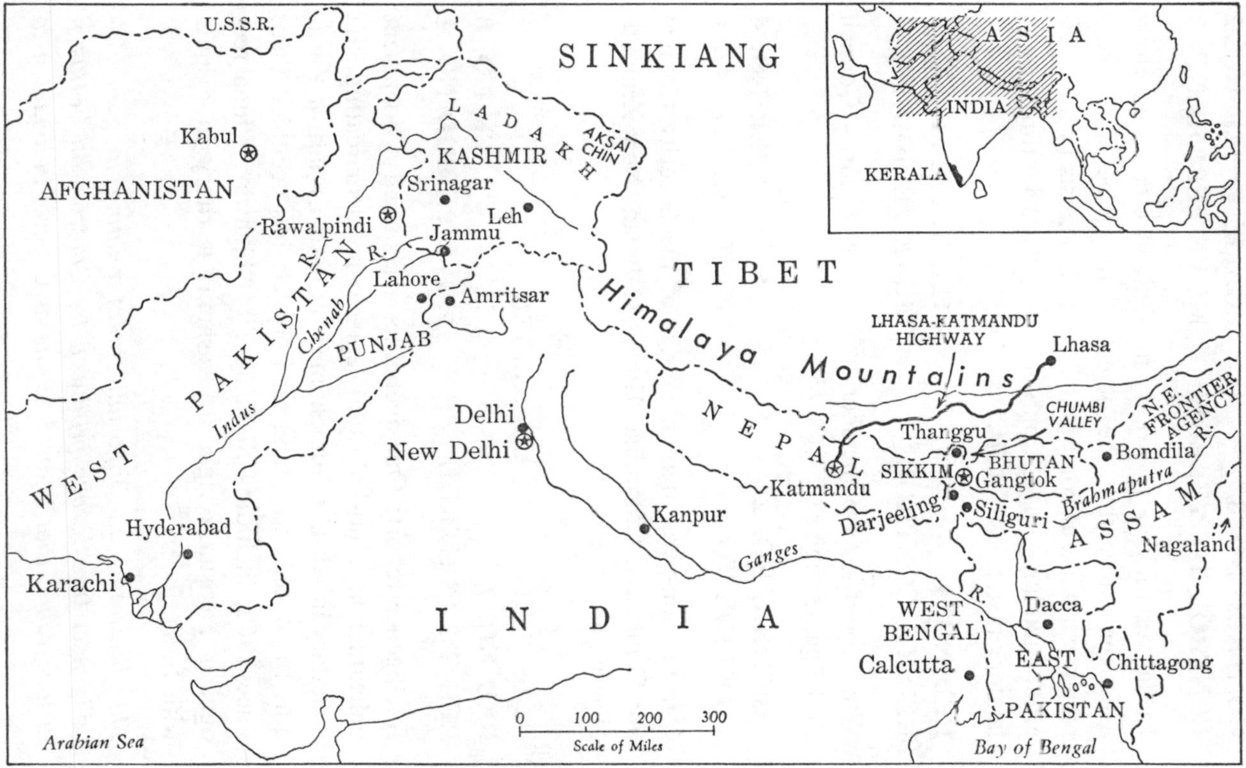
U.S.S.R.
SINKIANG
ASIA
INDIA
KERALA
AFGHANISTAN
Kabul
LADAKH
AKSAI CHIN
KASHMIR
Srinagar
Leh
Rawalpindi
Jammu
R.
Chenab
PUNJAB
Lahore
Amritsar
WEST PAKISTAN
Indus
TIBET
Himalaya Mountains
LHASA-KATMANDU HIGHWAY
Lhasa
CHUMBI VALLEY
N.E. FRONTIER AGENCY
Thanggu
BHUTAN
Bomdila
SIKKIM
Gangtok
Brahmaputra
R.
NEPAL
Katmandu
Darjeeling
Siliguri
ASSAM
Nagaland
Delhi
New Delhi
Kanpur
Ganges
Hyderabad
Karachi
INDIA
WEST BENGAL
Dacca
Calcutta
EAST PAKISTAN
Chittagong
0 100 200 300
Scale of Miles
Arabian Sea
Bay of Bengal

CONTROL NO. 1 **GAME PAPER NO. 2**
CONTROL TO YELLOW **MOVE PERIOD NO. 1**

In answer to Yellow No. 1, no limit to escalation. However, remember that the object of the game is to avoid major war without compromising vital interests (while preferably making gains). Confucius say: "He who throw away laundry ticket, loses shirt."

RED NO. 1 **GAME PAPER NO. 3**
RED TO CONTROL **MOVE PERIOD NO. 1**

What countries are members of the UN Security Council as the game begins?

CONTROL NO. 2 **GAME PAPER NO. 4**
CONTROL TO ALL **MOVE PERIOD NO. 1**

Current non-permanent members of the Security Council are Cambodia, Colombia, Hungary, Japan, New Zealand, Nigeria, and Portugal.

GAME
CLASSIFIED

RED NO. 2 **GAME PAPER NO. 8**
RED TO CONTROL **MOVE PERIOD NO. 1**

Intelligence report: Our agents have acquired a document indicating a Sino-Pakistani agreement demarcating the boundary in Aksai Chin, claimed by India as part of Kashmir, to concede to China territory she has occupied there since 1962, including Sinkiang-Tibet highway. China recognizes Pakistan's right to Kashmiri territory in dispute with India.

This illustrates an important point relating to game intelligence. Intelligence produced by Control can be taken at face value; that is, as accurate as Control indicates it to

132

be. But intelligence fabricated by a playing team cannot reliably be acted upon by that team unless and until it is confirmed by Control. In this instance, Red made an inspired guess. It required no confirmation from Control and received none.

GAME
CLASSIFIED

RED NO. 3	GAME PAPER NO. 9
RED TO CONTROL	**MOVE PERIOD NO. 1**

Situation Estimates and Objectives

Basic Objectives—(1) To maintain India as an effective obstacle to the expansion of the influence of the Chinese People's Republic (China) into South Asia, and to discredit its leaders even at the cost of collaboration with the United States. (2) If circumstances permit, to discredit the United States. (3) To prevent major war; i.e., involving the Soviet Union in war with either China or the United States, or the United States with China, and otherwise to limit hostilities to Indian border areas.

*Immediate Objectives—*Re-establish and maintain *status quo ante* (*i.e.,* prior to Pakistani offensive) with no penalties to Pakistan. Make clear to China the Soviet inability to remain indifferent in the event of Chinese expansionist moves.

Immediate Actions—

I. A public statement, released late September 1, reaffirms the established policy of the Soviet Union to oppose boundary changes by military action and calls on India and Pakistan to cease hostilities and negotiate differences.

II. Soviet troops in the Kirghiz and Tadzhik Socialist Soviet Republics, bordering China, are recalled to barracks.

133

It is assumed that this will be noted by Chinese intelligence.

Contingency Planning—The following mid-range contingencies were examined:

I. (Favorable Contingencies) Indian forces recover and appear likely to drive Pakistani invaders back to the truce line; Chinese involvement does not develop; there is a moderate increase in U.S. aid to India.

Proposed action: Support re-establishment of the previous truce line in Kashmir.

II. (Less Favorable Contingencies) Pakistan is successful in driving Indian forces out of Kashmir without active Chinese involvement; there are disastrous effects on Indian morale and public order; there is a moderate U.S. aid increase.

Proposed action: Call for a cease-fire to prevent spread of the war, and for a plebiscite to determine the future status of Kashmir.

III. (Still Less Favorable) Pakistan is initially successful and seems likely to gain control of Kashmir, with a threat of Indian counterattack against Pakistan proper. No overt Chinese involvement.

Proposed action: In the contingency that the United States supports an Indian counteroffensive, denounce India and the United States in the Security Council for aggression; demand a cease-fire and plebiscite in Kashmir. In the more likely event that the United States attempts to discourage an Indian counteroffensive against Pakistani territory, same except omit denunciation of the United States in the Security Council.

IV. (Serious Contingency) The Pakistani offensive is successful in Kashmir; overt Chinese support is limited to Kashmir, i.e., no movement of Chinese forces in the disputed border area of the North East Frontier Agency [NEFA]; there is a severe morale loss and threatened government instability in India; the United States substantially increases its military aid to India.

Proposed action: Denounce Pakistani aggression and Chinese imperialism; demand a cease-fire and the withdrawal of Pakistani and Chinese forces to restore the *status quo;* propose a UN force be dispatched to Kashmir to ensure restoration of the *status quo*—all actions in the Security Council.

V. (Worst Contingency) Same as IV above except that there are overt Chinese troop movements to occupy the demilitarized zone in the NEFA; general demoralization and disorder in India; massive U.S. aid short of combat units to India. The imminent possibility exists of a Chinese occupation of Nepal and Bhutan (perhaps by invitation of the local governments).

Proposed action: Same as in IV above plus reinforcement of Soviet troops on the Sinkiang border; increased diplomatic activity with Afghanistan and Mongolia; a military mission to India headed by Defense Minister. Open secret discussions with the United States regarding common problems connected with restoring the peace in Asia.

It should be noted that the Soviet team in developing "basic objectives" plainly regarded the Sino-Soviet split as irrevocable, for the statement contains no suggestion of a conciliatory move toward China.

GAME
CLASSIFIED

YELLOW NO. 2	**GAME PAPER NO. 10**
YELLOW TO CONTROL	**MOVE PERIOD NO. 1**

I. Objectives:

A. Chinese

1. Disrupt the Southeast Asia Treaty Organization (SEATO).

2. Improve own chances of United Nations membership.

3. Enhance China's military prestige.

4. Discredit Indian leadership and prestige, looking to eventual communization of India under Chinese tutelage.

5. Appeal for Afro-Asian support.

B. Pakistani

1. Improve prospects for a plebiscite on Kashmir.

2. Shift the military balance so as to assure Indian inability to crush Pakistan.

II. Contingent courses of action:

A. With respect to the United States:

If the United States increases the size of its military mission or logistical support, and/or sends high-level missions to India, China will reappraise the nature of the U.S. threat and consult with Pakistan.

If the United States significantly increases the level of its military aid to India, China will advance to attain the farthest defensible line within China-claimed territory before aid becomes effective. China will then proclaim a cease-fire and invite India to send a high-level delegation to Peking.

B. With respect to the United Kingdom:

If the United Kingdom increases its involvement in the crisis to any significant extent, China will apply pressure to Hong Kong, *e.g.*, by shutting off water. China will also secretly ask Indonesia to threaten Britain with increased action against Malaysia.

136

C. With respect to the Soviet Union:

If the Soviet Union sends military aid to India, China will denounce it through all available channels.

If the Soviet Union intensifies the Sino-Soviet border dispute, China will threaten Outer Mongolia.

D. With respect to the Republic of China (Taiwan):

If Taiwan involves itself in the crisis, China will intensify pressure against the offshore islands.

E. With respect to the United Nations:

If the crisis is taken to the United Nations, China will vociferously deny UN jurisdiction on the ground that such action is invalid unless China is seated in the United Nations. China will request that Cambodia take this line in the Security Council and support China's position in the crisis.

III. Immediate actions taken:

A. Military:

China to conduct aerial reconnaissance over New Delhi; increase military and logistical preparedness in all critical sectors; continue controlled and limited advances in Ladakh, NEFA, and Sikkim; and strengthen security forces in Tibet.

Pakistani forces in Kashmir to advance within the limits of logistic support and Indian resistance, and Pakistan to prepare for Indian counterattacks against East and West Pakistan.

B. Political:

China to invite India to hold bilateral talks in Peking; publicly claim to have received from Indian Communist sources a secret Indian Defense Ministry document indicating a plan to drive Chinese forces off all territory claimed by India and to link up with Tibetan guerrillas; China to use resident Indian Communists to conduct

137

psychological warfare against the Indian forces; and address propaganda to Afro-Asian nations stressing Indian aggression and China's peaceful intentions.

Pakistan to appeal for support of all Moslems, and to go to the United Nations with a charge of Indian refusal to hold a plebiscite in Kashmir and of Indian aggression against the Pakistani portion of Kashmir. Pakistan to appeal directly to the United States and the United Kingdom not to aid India.

The fifth item listed as a Chinese objective—"Appeal for Afro-Asian support"—is hardly an objective. Also, the contingent courses of action listed by the Sino-Pakistani team deal only with possible Chinese actions. Contingencies apparently won't affect Pakistan.

GAME
CLASSIFIED

BLUE NO. 2	**GAME PAPER NO. 11**
BLUE TO CONTROL	**MOVE PERIOD NO. 1**

U.S. Objectives:

1. Bring about a cease-fire in Kashmir with a return to the *status quo ante* of August 25, 1966.

2. Reinforce India against Chinese pressures on its northern borders; accomplish UN action to halt Chinese aggression if it becomes open and massive.

3. Produce a tolerable settlement of the Kashmir problem.

Indian Objectives:

1. Immediate withdrawal of Pakistani forces to behind the original, UN-patrolled cease-fire lines, i.e., of August 25.

2. Containment of the Communist Chinese advance into Sikkim and Aksai Chin.

3. Produce a favorable settlement of the Kashmir problem.

U.S.-Indian Contingency Plans:

1. If the Pakistani do not accept an ultimatum to halt their offensive by September 7, the United States will increase its military aid to India for use against Pakistan in Kashmir. The United States will also support an Indian appeal to the Security Council to intervene with a UN presence or military action if the Pakistani offensive continues beyond September 10.

2. If Pakistan accedes by September 7, the United States will make further assistance to India contingent upon India's willingness to accept UN arbitration of the Kashmir dispute. (Indian reservations are involved here.)

3. If the Chinese continue military action on the Indian border, the United States will support an Indian appeal to the United Nations to halt the aggression.

4. Enlist Soviet cooperation in pacifying the area. If this effort fails, and the Soviets muddy the water substantially, consider enlisting the cooperation of European allies in a NATO exercise and place the U.S. Strategic Air Command in a state of increased readiness. The above measures to be combined with a well-publicized build-up of U.S. forces at home, with initially small deployments toward the Far East. Design deployments to emphasize concern with China rather than with the Soviet Union.

5. India to resist aggression with vigorous military responses to the limit of the means available.

Immediate Actions:

A. Military:

1. Redeploy Pacific air and naval forces to strengthen the U.S. containment posture east and southeast of China.

2. Deploy U.S. naval aviation to the Bay of Bengal for use if Chinese forces enter India.

3. Alert the 3rd Marine Division at Okinawa for possible movement of elements thereof to Southeast Asia or South Korea.

4. Move two U.S. Air Force fighter squadrons (F-104) from the Philippines to Bangkok, Thailand.

B. Political:

1. Inform Pakistan that U.S. aid is to be held up until Pakistani forces return to the line of August 25; that major U.S. military aid will be extended to India if Pakistan does not comply by September 7; but that Pakistani compliance will produce U.S. support for prompt UN arbitration of the Kashmir dispute.

2. Inform India of the above démarche, adding that aid to India, if required by Chinese and Pakistani recalcitrance, will probably be conditional on Indian willingness to accept UN arbitration of the Kashmir dispute. Also, that the United States will not support Indian hostilities against Pakistan, if the latter withdraws as the United States has demanded.

3. Inform the Soviet Union that the United States is profoundly concerned with the Himalayan situation; that Pakistani aggression, with apparent Chinese support, threatens the outbreak of a major war affecting security interests of both the United States and the Soviet Union; that it is in their mutual interest to prevent any exploitation of the situation by the Chinese

140

and to encourage an immediate Pakistani-Indian cease-fire. Urge coordination of policy and action to this end, recognizing that the Soviet internal situation may require that cooperation be tacit and unacknowledged. Finally, inform the Soviets that the United States will view with the utmost gravity any Soviet moves tending to prolong or exacerbate the conflict in South Asia.

4. Inform allies, neutrals, and the United Nations, as appropriate, of the attitude and actions of the United States in respect to the situation in Kashmir and along the Sino-Indian border.

CONTROL NO. 5   **GAME PAPER NO. 12**
CONTROL TO ALL   **MOVE PERIOD NO. 2**

Second Move Scenario

During the first week of September 1966 the crisis in South Asia intensifies. By September 6 Pakistani forces have driven to the town of Srinagar, capturing the airfield there. The day earlier, Pakistan had already commenced an attack toward Jammu with the obvious objective of cutting off Indian reinforcements to Srinagar.

Meanwhile, Chinese forces are on the move. In the Ladakh area there is Chinese patrol action and small unit contact with Indian troops, but without conclusive results. The heaviest Chinese concentration, however, is in the Sikkim area. By September 6 Chinese forces have seized Gangtok and are advancing in the direction of Darjeeling. Indian forces are reported to be falling back slowly but in good order. In an effort to head off the Chinese advance, India has commenced an airlift of reserves into Siliguri.

Chinese moves in the NEFA area seem to be limited.

141

However, one clash between elements of a Chinese light division and Indian forces has been reported.

On September 2 five Chinese reconnaissance planes were sighted over New Delhi. Two of the aircraft were shot down by Indian F-104 interceptors. India, meanwhile, has launched its own reconnaissance sorties over Tibet.

On September 5 the Indian Air Force commenced interdiction attacks against Chinese troops and supply areas in the Chumbi Valley, Sikkim.

Against this military backdrop, there was frenzied diplomatic activity in the major capitals of the world.

Various statements were issued decrying the deteriorating situation in the Indian subcontinent and calling upon the principals to desist from armed hostilities. Among these was a statement by the Soviet Minister of Foreign Affairs asking India and Pakistan to cease fighting and to negotiate their differences. The Soviet Union stressed that it opposes any boundary changes by military action.

On September 2, India, charging that she is the victim of a flagrant and apparently concerted aggression on the parts of Pakistan and China, asked for immediate action by the United Nations. The Security Council met on the morning of September 4. After hearing charges and countercharges, the Council entertained a motion by the U.S. Ambassador calling for an immediate cease-fire between Pakistan and India, with withdrawal of Pakistani forces to the Kashmir truce line, the release by Pakistan of UN-Kashmir truce supervision teams, the acceptance by both India and Pakistan of UN arbitration, and the withdrawal of "foreign troops" from contested territory in northern India. After a debate during which the Soviet Union, among others, supported the U.S. proposal, France vetoed the motion.

142

The General Assembly, meanwhile, debated the issues, its deliberations bogged down by conflicting versions of what is happening. There appears to be a split among Afro-Asian delegations, the Moslem members urging a cautious approach to the problem and other "uncommitted" states avoiding a categorical stand. There appears to be a similar lack of unity among the Western delegations.

On September 4 China dispatched a communiqué to New Delhi, accusing India of aggression but reiterating its willingness to confer with India in order to resolve issues dividing the two countries. At the same time, the official Chinese News Agency issued a report that China had uncovered an Indian Defense Ministry document indicating Indian plans to expel Chinese forces from all territory claimed by India and to give material support to Tibetan "outlaws." The same edition carried an editorial alluding to attempts by a "powerful neighbor" of the Chinese People's Republic to exploit the crisis caused by Indian aggression, in order to threaten the territory of China. The editorial concluded that the Chinese People's Republic will firmly repel "any incursion from any source."

On September 5 Peking, reacting to the unfolding debate in the United Nations, issued a statement to the effect that, not being a member of the United Nations, the People's Republic rejects all attempts by the "alleged world organization" to inject itself into the territorial affairs of China.

On September 6 there is a flurry of international speculation over a front-page editorial in the Soviet party newspaper, *Pravda*. It denounced Pakistan for its obvious intent to take by force all of Kashmir in violation of existing statutes and international law. It demanded an immediate cease-fire in Kashmir and the withdrawal of all Pakistani forces behind the truce line. The main point of interest of the editorial, however, consisted of the harshest denunciation yet directed by the Soviet Union at Peking. Chinese action in India was described as "flagrant and unpardonable aggression departing from all accepted norms of Marxist-Leninist legality." The editorial documented this accusation with "reliable information" respecting the existence of a Chinese-Pakistani agreement for a joint conquest of territory at the expense of India.

On September 6, following the French veto in the Security Council and obvious indecision in the General Assembly, Secretary General U Thant invoked his broad powers based upon the earlier, vaguely worded UN mandate on Kashmir and dispatched from Cyprus two charter airplanes carrying UN observers. He issued communiqués to Pakistan and India advising of the imminent arrival of these "UN aircraft," requesting landing rights for the planes in Lahore and Amritsar, respectively, and safe conduct of the teams to the area of hostilities.

It is now September 7, 1966 (pick your time).

GAME
CLASSIFIED

CONTROL NO. 6	**GAME PAPER NO. 13**
CONROL TO RED	**MOVE PERIOD NO. 2**

Red Addendum to Second Move Scenario

On September 3 Soviet troops in the Kirghiz and Tadzhik Republics were recalled to barracks.

The U.S. Ambassador in Moscow informed the Soviet Foreign Minister of profound U.S. concern over increasing tension and localized conflicts in the Himalayan area. Apparent major Pakistani aggression in Kashmir was held to threaten the outbreak of a wider war, ultimately affecting security interests of both the United States and the Soviet

Union. The Ambassador expressed his belief that it was in the mutual interest of the United States and the Soviet Union to prevent Chinese exploitation of the situation in South Central Asia. He expressed the hope that the Soviet Union would encourage a cease-fire in the Kashmir conflict, and that the Soviet Union would openly engage in common action to this end. He stated, however, that the United States would understand if the internal political situation in the Soviet Union demanded that any such cooperation be tacit and unacknowledged. The Soviet reaction was friendly but noncommittal.

On September 4 Soviet intelligence reported Chinese troop mobilizations in regions adjacent to the Mongolian People's Republic. The movement coincided with an inflammatory Chinese editorial of the same date.

On September 6 the U.S. Ambassador again called at the Foreign Ministry. He stated that he had been instructed by Washington to convey to the Soviet Union the fact that the United States had been forced by the evolution of events in South Asia "to take certain preparatory actions of a strategic nature" in the Pacific and Indian Ocean areas. The Ambassador stressed that these were strictly defensive measures and were in no way directed at the Soviet Union.

By September 5 there have been harried meetings in East European capitals, with strong concern voiced at the danger of an imminent Sino-Soviet confrontation over the conflict in India. On September 6 Soviet Premier Kosygin received a personal message from Polish First Secretary Gomulka, asserting that the latter spoke "for the great majority" of members of the Socialist camp and the world Communist movement in urging the Soviet Union to refrain from any action which might cause a permanent rupture with the Chinese People's Republic.

GAME
CLASSIFIED

CONTROL NO. 7   GAME PAPER NO. 14
CONTROL TO BLUE   MOVE PERIOD NO. 2

Blue Addendum to Second Move Scenario

On September 2 the U.S. Ambassador in Rawalpindi informed the Pakistani Government that U.S. military and economic aid has been stopped until Pakistani forces return to the line occupied by them on August 25. He conveyed the warning that, if the withdrawal was not effected by September 7, the United States would give "immediate assistance to India commensurate with the situation." The U.S. Ambassador promised that the U.S. Government would urge the United Nations to review and arbitrate the Kashmir dispute if Pakistani forces did withdraw.

On September 2 the U.S. Ambassador in New Delhi informed the Indian Government of the U.S. démarche at Rawalpindi, adding that the United States is ready to funnel substantial aid to India if Pakistani forces do not withdraw or if Chinese attacks continue. The Ambassador, however, attached to the prospect of such aid the proviso that India agree to accept UN arbitration of the Kashmir dispute. As of September 6 there has been no reply from India, New Delhi apparently awaiting a Pakistani reaction to the U.S. deadline.

The United States has informed Turkey, Thailand, the Philippines, Afghanistan, Iran, and Nationalist China of its concern regarding the situation in India, reassuring these countries that it will meet all commitments toward them and requesting intransit and overflight rights in the event that a U.S. movement of military aid to the Indian subcon-

146

tinent becomes necessary. To the latter request only the Philippines and Thailand have reacted positively.

On September 3 orders were given to U.S. forces in the Indian Ocean and Western Pacific to prepare themselves for possible action. The U.S. Concord Squadron (carrier task force), then off the coast of East Africa, was ordered to move into the Bay of Bengal. The 7th Fleet was ordered to increase its readiness in the Taiwan area. The 3rd Marine Division at Okinawa was alerted for possible deployment to South Korea or Southeast Asia. U.S. tactical aircraft were ordered to Bangkok. Nationalist Chinese naval and air force units were alerted for possible action. Nationalist Chinese reconnaissance planes became especially active over the Fukien coast of Communist China, reporting increasing military activities opposite the offshore islands.

On September 3 the U.S. Ambassador in Moscow informed the Soviet Foreign Minister of profound U.S. concern over increasing tension and localized conflict in the Himalayan area. He stated that Pakistani aggression in Kashmir threatens a wider war, ultimately affecting security interests of both the United States and the Soviet Union. The Ambassador also expressed his government's belief that the two countries share a mutual interest in preventing the exploitation of the situation by China in South Central Asia or elsewhere. The Ambassador hoped that the Soviet Union would encourage a cease-fire in the Kashmir conflict. He urged open U.S.-Soviet coordination of policies to these ends, but said his government would understand if the internal political situation in the Soviet Union demanded that such cooperation be tacit and unacknowledged. The Soviet reaction was friendly but guarded.

On September 5 the U.S. Embassy in Moscow reported

persistent rumors of Soviet and Chinese military incidents in Sinkiang and Outer Mongolia.

Western sources in Eastern European capitals report obvious restiveness, punctuated by top-level Communist Party meetings, reflecting apparent fear of a complete Sino-Soviet rupture or even of a Sino-Soviet military confrontation.

On September 3 in Washington, Secretary of State Dean Rusk summoned the British Ambassador to discuss the possible extent of British cooperation in the event that military action against China and/or Pakistan should be required. The Ambassador expressed the extreme reluctance of the British Government to become directly involved in a conflict between two members of the Commonwealth. With regard to the possible U.S. use of British air bases in Malaysia, or elsewhere, he suggested that such bases might be made available only if other alternatives for U.S. access were wholly barred.

Elements in the Pakistani Government are reported toying with the idea, inferred from the U.S. démarche of September 2, that a withdrawal by Pakistan from present military positions in Kashmir might secure U.S. support for a plebiscite solution to the Kashmir problem.

GAME
CLASSIFIED

CONTROL NO. 8	**GAME PAPER NO. 15**
CONTROL TO YELLOW	**MOVE PERIOD NO. 2**

Yellow Addendum to Second Move Scenario

On September 2 the United States informed Pakistan that U.S. military and economic aid had been stopped until Pakistani forces returned to the line occupied before August 25. The United States warned that if Pakistan did not comply by September 7, it would give immediate aid to India "commensurate with the situation." The U.S. Ambassador promised that, if Pakistan did comply, the United States would urge UN review and arbitration of the Kashmir dispute.

On September 3 Chinese intelligence reported that Soviet garrisons in the Kirghiz and Tadzhik Republics had been recalled to their barracks.

On September 3, evaluating newspaper reports concerning an urgent meeting between U.S. Secretary of State Dean Rusk and the British Ambassador in Washington, Chinese intelligence suggested that the United States had asked for common U.S.-British action in India, and estimated that the British would be reluctant to become involved.

On September 4 intelligence reports poured in about increasing activity of the U.S. 7th Fleet in the Taiwan Straits; about the ready alert of Chinese Nationalist naval and air forces; and about the stepped-up pace of U-2 intelligence flights over Communist China.

On September 4 China mobilized troops on its territory adjacent to the Republic of Outer Mongolia. That same day Peking gave orders to its agents in India to agitate against Indian military efforts and, in general, attempt to hamper Indian mobilization efforts. Agents report moderate success in this endeavor and the low morale of Indian troops.

Intelligence from Eastern Europe, toward the end of the week, reports intense restiveness in East European capitals and fears of a Sino-Soviet confrontation. Unconfirmed reports suggest that Gomulka of Poland may have personally communicated this concern to Moscow.

Elements in the Pakistani Government are reported toying with the idea, inferred from the U.S. démarche, that a

149

unilateral withdrawal by them from Kashmir might secure for them American support for a plebiscite in Kashmir.

It will be noted that the Control team, in its projection of the scenario toward a second move period, has generally stayed within the limits of contingency situations and actions described by the three playing teams in their first move papers. True, the contingent situations developed are hardly the most favorable envisaged by the teams, and in fact verge on the worst possibilities they considered. This is well designed to move the crisis along.

Control has, as requested, introduced suggestions of independent action by both India and Pakistan. Control has also produced several additional developments. The Secretary General of the United Nations is taking somewhat questionable initiatives of his own, including a dispatch of UN aircraft to India and Pakistan without bothering to obtain landing permissions. The East European Communist states are represented as giving the Soviets considerable trouble. France has vetoed a proposal in the Security Council supported by the Soviet Union as well as by the United States and Great Britain.

The French veto was apparently regarded by some players as an especially contrary action on the part of President Charles de Gaulle, for the glory of France. Challenges produced the explanation that follows.

CONTROL NO. 12 **GAME PAPER NO. 21**
CONTROL TO ALL **MOVE PERIOD NO. 2**

Re the French veto of September 4 on the U.S. motion in the Security Council:

The delegate of France elaborated his government's position to the effect that, although France joins others in the desire for peace in the Indian subcontinent, it reiterates its position, dating back to the 1960 UN interference in the Congo, that the United Nations exceeds its mandate by flagrant intervention in the internal affairs of member nations. He added pointedly that the motion in question was addressed also to the Chinese People's Republic which, not being a member of the United Nations, was not in a position to defend itself against the implications of the motion.

CONTROL NO. 13   GAME PAPER NO. 22
CONTROL TO ALL   MOVE PERIOD NO. 2

As of September 7 there are reports of increasing agitation in Western Europe regarding the implications of a rumored U.S.-Soviet agreement regarding a concert of purpose in the South Asia crisis, as presaged by their common action in the United Nations.

Typical is the following editorial comment from the *Frankfurter Allgemeine:* "Can the United States maintain a credible deterrent against Soviet aggression in Europe— credible to Western Europe as well as to the Soviet Union— at the same time that it makes common cause with the Soviets in other areas of the world?"

New subject: Within India, communal and other rioting and disorder is being brought under reasonable control.

The teams, during their second move, produced papers which again permitted Control to project the scenario forward, without doing too much violence to team intentions, for the third and final move of the game.

CONTROL NO. 14   GAME PAPER NO. 26
CONTROL TO ALL   MOVE PERIOD NO. 3

Third Move Scenario

The tense crisis in the Indian subcontinent continued into the second week of September 1966. On the military front there were major developments.

In Kashmir, Pakistani forces were beginning to attack Indian units south of Srinagar. Indian forces were falling back slowly under pressure, but shortages of ammunition and other supplies were a serious handicap to Indian defense operations. The Indian commander in Sikkim reported that Chinese forces had apparently broken off the attack and were preparing defensive positions. Farther east, in the NEFA area, Chinese forces continued to press attacks toward Bomdila. However, Indian forces were relinquishing ground grudgingly and the Chinese advance was slow. The Indian commander estimated, on September 12, that he could delay a Chinese seizure of Bomdila for two to three weeks.

At the same time, there was increased Chinese military activity in Ladakh. The Indian commander there informed New Delhi that only immediate reinforcements could prevent a Chinese seizure of Leh. In Dacca, East Pakistan, on September 10, the Pakistani Air Force reported shooting down two Indian reconnaissance planes.

Meanwhile, U.S. strategic preparations in the Western Pacific and Indian Ocean areas continued. On September 9 the U.S. Indian Ocean carrier task force (Concord Squadron) entered the Bay of Bengal. On the same day, elements of the 3rd U.S. Marine Division arrived in Bangkok.

There were reports, fragmentary and unconfirmed, of

stepped-up Soviet military activity in Central Asia along the Sino-Soviet border.

The intensification of the crisis was reflected at the same time in various developments on the diplomatic and political front.

On September 7 President Johnson held a press conference to discuss the growing gravity of the problems resulting from Pakistani military actions in Kashmir and from Chinese actions on the northern borders. He indicated the belief that two distinct crises have resulted. The President expressed his regret at the failure to make effective use of the great potential of the United Nations. He pledged U.S. support of Secretary General U Thant in his efforts to pacify the situation by dispatching UN observers into the area. The President said further that, although the United States hopes for and will do all in its power to achieve a peaceful settlement, he has authorized that U.S. forces in the Pacific be placed in an increased state of readiness and deployed in areas where they may be available to cope with any contingencies threatening the security of free nations in South Asia. He announced that he is calling a meeting of Congressional leaders of both parties to review the situation.

Early in the morning of September 7 an aircraft carrying a UN fact-finding mission set down at Lahore airport. The team was met by a group of high-ranking Pakistani officials at the head of an honor guard, escorted to waiting buses and driven off.

At the same time, a second aircraft carrying UN observers landed at Amritsar, India. The team went into immediate consultation with waiting Indian officials. The latter pledged complete cooperation, but expressed their concern that Pakistani aggression in Kashmir had rendered access

to the area extremely difficult. The team cabled UN headquarters in New York, asking that immediate permission be
requested from Pakistan for landing rights and safe conduct
for the team into and from Srinagar airfield.

On the evening of September 7 in the United States, the
Huntley-Brinkley report noted rumors in Washington that
the Congress would shortly pass a joint resolution authoriz-
ing whatever action the President deems necessary. Senator
Everett Dirksen, in an interview, stated that the United
States "cannot fail to demonstrate its national courage" and
"must be boldly discreet in coming to the aid of victims of
an infamous aggression."

Early on September 8 President Johnson left Washington
for Johnson City, Texas.

On September 8 in Rawalpindi there was increasing confusion regarding the UN fact-finding team to Pakistan,
which had not been heard of since landing at Lahore. To
persistent inquiries, a Pakistani spokesman finally indicated
that the team was being "thoroughly briefed" on the situation in Kashmir before being escorted to the scene of
hostilities. He said that he could not reveal the present
whereabouts of the UN mission because the Pakistani Secret
Service had uncovered a plot by fanatic Hindus against the
lives of the UN representatives.

On September 8 in New Delhi reports from various
sections of India suggested that communal violence apparently will subside unless Communist internal agitation is
strongly renewed.

In Peking on September 8 Premier Chou En-lai issued a
statement regarding "certain skirmishes" between units of
the Chinese People's Republic and forces "in the pay of the
reactionary Indian bourgeoisie." He stressed that, despite
provocations suffered by China, its intentions are peaceful

and that "redressive action" has been undertaken by China solely in response to Indian aggression. Such action had also been reluctantly taken in Sikkim as the result of Indian provocations. The people of Sikkim were "welcoming the valiant troops of the Chinese People's Republic" as liberators from Indian aggression.

On September 9 President Johnson returned to Washington from Johnson City.

On September 9 the heads of state of major East European countries converged on Moscow for a hastily convened meeting of the Warsaw Pact. Conspicuous by his absence was the Rumanian First Party Secretary. The purpose of the meeting was not announced, but it seemed clearly to be connected with reported restiveness in Eastern Europe regarding the growing Sino-Soviet confrontation over events in South Asia.

On September 9 President Ayub Khan of Pakistan held a press conference in which he reiterated charges that Indian provocations in Kashmir had necessitated Pakistani military action. He denied Soviet allegations that the Pakistani moves had been either premeditated or staged in concert with another power. President Ayub Khan indicated that, despite India's aggressiveness, he stood ready to order the withdrawal of Pakistani forces from positions beyond the cease-fire line, provided that India immediately agree to a plebiscite in Kashmir under UN auspices.

On September 9 the New China News Agency in Peking attributed to a high official in the Communist Chinese Government the statement that a solution to the chronic problem along the Sino-Indian border would "probably be facilitated" if the Chinese People's Republic were to take its rightful place in the United Nations.

While the Warsaw Pact meeting was still in progress on

155

September 10, Soviet Defense Minister Malinovsky, heading a delegation of Soviet military, embarked from Moscow airport for New Delhi.

In Karachi and elsewhere, on September 10, speculation continued regarding the whereabouts of the UN fact-finding mission to Pakistan.

On September 10 two squadrons of American F-104 fighters left Clark Air Force Base in the Philippines en route to India. Their movement coincided with an announcement by U.S. Secretary of Defense Robert McNamara that a "substantial U.S. military assistance effort to India" had commenced.

In New York on the afternoon of September 10, UN Secretary General U Thant convened a press conference. After alluding to the deepening crisis in South Asia and its very real threat to world peace, he dropped what reporters called a "bombshell." He was convinced, said the Secretary General, that a "durable resolution" of the crisis must have as its prerequisite the admission of the Chinese People's Republic into the United Nations. He added that he had taken soundings among UN delegations and believed it to be "by far the majority sentiment" that the Chinese People's Republic be admitted to the United Nations and to China's seat in the Security Council, with Taiwan retaining membership in the General Assembly. When asked by reporters whether Communist China would now accept a "two-China" formula, U Thant replied that only Peking can answer this question.

On September 11 Radio Moscow interrupted a program on Kazak culture with the announcement that the India-bound aircraft carrying Marshal Malinovsky was reported missing. The plane had last reported while over the treacherous Pamirs mountain range of the Soviet Union. Search planes have been dispatched to the area, it reported, but unfavorable weather plus the forbidding terrain precluded hopes for early results.

September 11 press reports in Western Europe reflected continuing and growing anxiety regarding an "evolving U.S.-Soviet partnership" in South Asia.

On the morning of September 11 Ambassador George McGhee met in Bonn with West German Chancellor Erhardt. Reliable sources in Bonn suggested that the Ambassador had explained to Chancellor Erhardt the U.S. policy in South Asia, but that the Chancellor had apparently not been reassured.

On September 12, amid growing conviction that the aircraft carrying Marshal Malinovsky and his delegation to New Delhi had indeed crashed, the somber-faced Soviet Ambassador to India held a two-hour meeting in New Delhi with Prime Minister Shastri and high-ranking members of the Indian military. Prime Minister Shastri subsequently called a press conference in which he described the general military situation, particularly the plight of Indian forces in Kashmir. Of greater import were two statements by the Prime Minister. He said that India now stands ready to accept UN arbitration of the Kashmir controversy, but would do so only if all—and he stressed "all"—foreign forces now in India had returned to the positions which they occupied prior to September 1. Secondly, Shastri reported what he called a "concrete and substantial offer of Soviet military assistance to India if encroachments upon Indian territory did not cease immediately."

On September 12 Pakistani Government sources reported growing disorder and sabotage in East Pakistan, provoked by Indian agents and Hindu elements.

The same day President Johnson left Washington for

Johnson City, taking the entire National Security Council with him.

It is now September 13, 1966.

GAME
CLASSIFIED

CONTROL NO. 15   GAME PAPER NO. 27
CONTROL TO BLUE   MOVE PERIOD NO. 3

Blue Addendum to Third Move Scenario

On September 8, replying to the U.S. communication regarding impending aid to India and requesting clarification of Pakistan's demand for a plebiscite, the Pakistani Government said:

1. Pakistan understands that the United States has commitments to India to give military assistance against China's "aggression," but deplores the fact that this aid has in the past been, and is now being, used by India against Pakistan. Pakistan welcomes, therefore, U.S. assurance that the Kashmir incident and the so-called Chinese "aggressions" are being considered separately, and expects that the United States will not tolerate the use of any aid it may give to India against the rightful self-defense measures of Pakistan. If India uses such equipment in further aggressions against Pakistan, the government will be obliged to seek immediate military aid for its own defense.

2. Regarding the distinction between a plebiscite, which Pakistan is demanding for Kashmir, and UN arbitration, which the U.S. says it is urging India to accept, the position of the Pakistani Government is as follows: Arbitration, under UN or any other auspices, is not acceptable to Pakistan and to the people of Kashmir because it fails to accord the latter their right to self-determination. As there is no guarantee that "arbitration," whether conducted in or out of the

United Nations, would be productive of a true and acceptable solution, the Pakistani Government insists that the people of Kashmir be allowed to express their political preference in a fair and impartially supervised plebiscite. Only by granting to the several million Kashmiris the fundamental right of self-determination, so convincingly enunciated in the Fourteen Points, the Atlantic Charter, and the Charter of the United Nations, can continuing Kashmiri injustices be brought to an end.

3. Pakistan appreciates the U.S. warning regarding the danger of a Chinese presence in the subcontinent, but sees no imminent threat to its own safety from this quarter. China has in the past behaved most correctly vis-à-vis Pakistan, and there are no outstanding issues in dispute between them.

On September 10, in reply to the U.S. communication to India on the subject, the Indian Government stated that it unilaterally accepts UN arbitration of the Kashmir dispute, provided all aggressive forces are withdrawn behind the lines of September 1. A public announcement to this effect was also made by the Prime Minister on September 11.

In an aside to the U.S. Ambassador, however, Indian officials stated categorically that they looked to the United States, which had involved itself with Pakistan, to bring about the withdrawal of Pakistani aggressor forces to the pre-attack lines. India could not compel Pakistan to retreat without extending and intensifying the conflict.

(The United States considered this Indian declaration as fulfilling the conditions for extending aid to India. Aid was begun on September 11. The U.S. mission immediately began preparations for additional aid on the basis of talks already begun with Indian staff officials.)

India again indicated its willingness to support the admission of Communist China to the United Nations as a price for restoring stability at this critical moment.

Later on September 10 Ambassador Chester Bowles in New Delhi reported that the Indian Government had informed him of evidence that China is involved in spreading communal disorders and that India wished to invoke the promise of an earlier communication for immediate U.S. aid. The Indians ask for riot control weapons (including armored personnel carriers and some light arms) in order to increase the effectiveness of police units and thereby free regular troops presently tied down.

Also on September 10 the United Nations Ambassador reported that the Secretary General has told him he will later that same day announce his proposal to have Communist China admitted to the United Nations, replacing Nationalist China in the Security Council. In informal consultations, the Secretary General has ascertained that the proposal will be actively supported by the Soviet Union, India, Pakistan, France, and a large majority of the uncommitted nations.

On September 11 Ambassador George McGhee reported from Bonn Chancellor Erhardt's reaction to his conveyed assurances as being discouraging. While Erhardt did not doubt that the United States had the best intentions, he did not conceal the fact that he considered U.S. actions, particularly the close U.S.-Soviet cooperation, disastrous for himself, for his government, and possibly for NATO as well. He pointed out that there were strong pressures within his own party, and pressures from France within the alliance, urging him to repudiate those U.S. actions which diminished the credibility of the U.S. deterrent in Europe. Erhardt pointed out that these sources threatened to deny him their support in matters of common policy and that this was putting him in a position of having to choose between Washington and Europe. He would soon be faced with a serious domestic crisis as well, if U.S. actions continued to confirm the predictions of Gaullist factions in Europe.

On September 11, replying to a U.S. inquiry, the Soviets informed Washington of their military moves along the China border and of the formation of Kazak militia units. The Soviet Ambassador conveyed his government's willingness to conduct talks between the U.S. Department of Defense and the Soviet Ministry of Defense regarding possible joint undertakings in this crisis. The Ambassador said that the Soviet Ambassador in Peking had finally been received by the Chinese Politburo on September 8, but gave no details of the meeting.

The Soviet Ambassador was informed by the State Department as to U.S. diplomatic moves in Pakistan and India, and the Soviet Union was asked to join with the United States in guaranteeing the safety of the UN team dispatched by U Thant. The State Department said it wished to ascertain the extent to which the Soviet Government might be willing to coordinate action aimed at preventing further incursions by China in areas claimed by India. The Soviet Ambassador said that his government would inform the United States of its decisions in this respect.

In New Delhi the Soviet Ambassador urged the Indian Government to block the Lhasa-Katmandu Highway and expressed understanding of the possible need for India to occupy parts of East Pakistan.

GAME
CLASSIFIED

CONTROL NO. 16	GAME PAPER NO. 28
CONTROL TO RED	MOVE PERIOD NO. 3

Red Addendum to Third Move Scenario

During the Warsaw Pact meeting in Moscow, on September 8, Soviet representatives stressed that China is risking destruction in a war with the United States. Therefore, they said, the Soviet Union tries to preserve, rather than to split, the Socialist camp by discouraging Chinese military moves in India. A limited U.S.-Soviet collaboration is necessary to avert disaster for the Socialist camp.

On September 11 the Soviet Government urged the Indian Government to block the Lhasa-Katmandu Highway and expressed its understanding of the possible need for occupation of parts of East Pakistan by India.

Also on September 11 the Soviet Ambassador in Washington informed the State Department of Soviet moves along its Chinese border, the formation of Kazak militia units, and suggested confidential contacts between the U.S. Department of Defense and the Soviet Ministry of Defense. He also informed the U.S. Government that the Soviet Ambassador in Peking had been received by the Politburo of the Chinese People's Republic on September 8, but revealed no details concerning the talks.

The Soviet Ambassador in Peking in fact outlined the position of his government to the Chinese Politburo. He pointed out the danger of war between China and the United States, stressing U.S. nuclear superiority over China, and explained that Soviet military moves on its boundaries with China are designed to preserve as much of China as possible in the Socialist camp should there eventuate a U.S.-Chinese

162

war. The Soviet Ambassador also mentioned reports that the Pakistani Government would entertain the idea of withdrawing its forces from Kashmir in return for the assurance of a plebiscite solution. The Soviet Government urged the Chinese Government to support restoration of the Kashmir truce line and to withdraw those Chinese forces which had advanced beyond the boundary claimed by China in 1962. It promised support to China in obtaining its 1962-claimed boundary in a final settlement.

The United States, on September 11, informed the Soviet Ambassador in Washington of U.S. diplomatic moves in Pakistan and in India. The Soviet Union was asked to join in guaranteeing the safety of the UN teams dispatched by U Thant on September 6, and to assist India with material aid in repulsing Pakistani and Chinese incursions into Indian territory. The Soviet Government fully accepted an exchange of information and possible coordination of shipments of aid.

GAME
CLASSIFIED

CONTROL NO. 17   GAME PAPER NO. 29
CONTROL TO YELLOW   MOVE PERIOD NO. 3

Yellow Addendum to Third Move Scenario

The Soviet Government and the government of Outer Mongolia were told through semi-official channels that, if the Soviets permit any military incidents on the Chinese border, China would consider occupying certain areas in Mongolia vital to its own security. Well-informed sources reported from Ulan Bator (Outer Mongolia) that Kazakstan militia units are apparently being formed, traitors who have been leaving Sinkiang in the last five years being encouraged to join these units.

163

The Chinese Embassy in Moscow reports that, in the meeting of the Warsaw Pact on September 8, Soviet representatives have taken the position that further involvement of China in South Asia would lead to its destruction by the United States and thus to a crippling blow for the whole Socialist camp. Soviet representatives argued that it was therefore in China's interest that the Soviet Union has been trying to halt Chinese operations on the Indian border. East European delegates expressed their dissatisfaction with the course of action taken by the Soviet Government. They voiced their objections to cooperation between the Soviet Union and the United States in the present conflict and expressed their misgivings about its consequences for the unity and strength of the Socialist camp as well as for future developments in Europe.

Rumors are reported in New Delhi as indicating that the Soviet Government has encouraged India to initiate moves against Pakistan and in the Himalayas.

After several requests, the Soviet Ambassador in Peking was invited to meet on September 8 with the Politburo. During the conference he stressed the gravity of the situation and strongly urged that China heed Soviet warnings. The Ambassador protested "aggressive" Chinese actions against India, pointing to the danger of a major war between China and the United States, and expressed Soviet unwillingness to involve the Socialist camp as a whole in such a war. The Ambassador said that the Soviet Government was confident that China could not survive nuclear attack by the United States and that precautionary Soviet military moves on its China border are designed solely to enable the Soviet Union to preserve as much of China in the Socialist camp as possible in the event of such a war. The Ambassador called the attention of the Politburo to unconfirmed reports that the

Pakistani Government is receptive to the idea of withdrawing its forces from Kashmir in return for assurance of a plebiscite solution. The Soviet Government urged China to support a restoration of Kashmir's truce line and to withdraw Chinese forces that have advanced into Kashmir or India beyond boundaries claimed by China in 1962. The Soviet Government at the same time promised its support of the Chinese boundary claims of 1962 in a final settlement with India.

GAME
CLASSIFIED

YELLOW NO. 4 **GAME PAPER NO. 30**
YELLOW TO CONTROL **MOVE PERIOD NO. 3**

I. Chinese Moves:

A. Military

Communist China stops its advance in Ladakh short of its claimed frontier; consolidates its position in Sikkim without reinforcing; and continues its controlled advance in NEFA.

B. Political

Communist China announces that its forces are not on Indian territory; again proposes bilateral negotiations with India on the territorial dispute; announces it will withdraw to pre-September 1 positions in Sikkim after a Kashmir plebiscite; states again that a "two Chinas" arrangement is unacceptable, but invites Secretary General U Thant to Peking to discuss the question of Chinese representation in the United Nations; assures the Soviet Union that no war with the United States is desired; requests an ambassadorial meeting with the United States in Warsaw and publishes a statement to this effect; and publicly protests U.S. military moves in the Indian Ocean and Thailand.

II. Pakistani Moves:

A. Military

Pakistani forces continue their limited advances in Kashmir.

B. Political

Pakistan reiterates its demand for a Kashmir plebiscite; facilitates the movement of the UN truce team in Pakistan to Kashmir; but denies entry to Kashmir to the UN truce team in India.

GAME
CLASSIFIED

RED NO. 6   **GAME PAPER NO. 31**
RED TO CONTROL   **MOVE PERIOD NO. 3**

Meetings with East European Prime Ministers are continuing. At a session today they will be told: (1) The Soviet Government suspects that the aircraft carrying Defense Minister Malinovsky to New Delhi was shot down by Chinese interceptor fighters. (2) It is becoming clear what Communist Chinese and Pakistani primary objectives are: to force entry of the former into the United Nations and to achieve a settlement of the Kashmir dispute by plebiscite, tantamount to Indian surrender of its claims. (3) Conversations with the United States are continuing, with a complete meeting of minds on the necessity of limiting conflict and forestalling aggressive objectives by force of arms. (4) Troop lift is standing by at Tashkent to move an airborne division to India if requested; the U.S. Government has been informed of this move. (5) The Soviet Ambassador in Peking will inform Communist China that the Soviet Union is not prepared in current circumstances to support its admission to the United Nations; the U.S. Government is being confidentially informed of this position and is expected to cooperate in preventing the issue from coming to a vote.

Actions vis-à-vis Communist China: The Soviet Ambassador is instructed to inform Peking that the Soviet Union is prepared to respond favorably to an Indian request for direct military assistance if U.S. reinforcements are deemed by India inadequate to contain the Chinese thrusts into Ladakh and the NEFA. The Ambassador is to state that the situation has already gone beyond any tolerable stress upon relations between the two leading Socialist countries, and that steps must be taken to reverse the trend or the consequences will be a disaster for Marxism-Leninism. The Ambassador is to conclude that the Soviet Union does not presently feel itself in a position to support Communist Chinese claims to UN membership. Some grave questions as to the Malinovsky disaster exist in Moscow.

Actions vis-à-vis India: The Soviet Ambassador in New Delhi, meeting with Prime Minister Shastri on September 13, protests indications of Indian willingness to accept UN arbitration of the Kashmir dispute, pointing out that this is tantamount to surrender to Pakistan at the point of a gun, and that this will also constitute an unqualified victory for a Communist China currently engaged in aggression against Indian territory. The Soviet Government is prepared to contribute forces, starting with one airborne division to Ladakh within three days. The Ambassador urges that Prime Minister Shastri reopen the issue of Sino-Pakistani aggressive action in the United Nations and that he propose, possibly through a friendly African intermediary, the immediate movement to India of UN forces, to include U.S. and Soviet forces.

Actions vis-à-vis the United States: The Ambassador is to

167

reconfirm Soviet understanding of the U.S. action in sending fighter aircraft to India. The Ambassador will state the Soviet preference that U.S. and Soviet forces assisting India be incorporated in a UN peace-keeping force. Failing Security Council action to this end, perhaps in consequence of French intransigeance, the Soviet Union will understand unilateral U.S. action, particularly as the Indian Government would almost certainly then request Soviet troops also. The U.S. Government is urged to apply all possible pressure on Paris to prevent a repetition of the veto should the UN force issue be raised by or for India.

GAME

CLASSIFIED

BLUE NO. 5	**GAME PAPER NO. 32**
BLUE TO CONTROL	**MOVE PERIOD NO. 3**

President Johnson addressed the nation on the night of September 13, indicating that the crisis in South Asia continues unabated. While the United States is doing all it can to achieve a peaceful settlement, it is also increasing aid to India to meet the double crisis on its northern border. The U.S. Government, he continued, appreciates the efforts of Secretary General U Thant to achieve a peaceful settlement. However, it disagrees that Communist China's admission to the United Nations will solve the crisis, and will continue to oppose its admission to the Security Council. If Communist China demonstrates good faith by withdrawing all forces to the lines of August 25, and immediately accedes to a nuclear test-ban treaty, the United States will not discourage General Assembly consideration of the admission of Communist China to that body.

The President announced that two squadrons of F-104 fighter aircraft are now in India, that a U.S. carrier task force has entered the Bay of Bengal, and that elements of the 3rd U.S. Marine Division have arrived in Bangkok. These forces stand ready at once, he said, to assist in repelling aggression against India.

Actions Taken:

Cable to U.S. Ambassador, Pakistan: Convey the following to the Pakistani Government: The United States is concerned at Pakistani failure to understand the distinction between arbitration and mediation. The U.S. Government sympathizes with Pakistan's refusal to continue the long and fruitless series of advisory findings and efforts at mediation. Pakistan should understand that acceptance of arbitration constitutes an advance acceptance of the findings of the arbitrating body. India has already agreed to this. Pakistan must surely realize that ethnic and religious factors in Kashmir make it highly likely that any impartial body will reach conclusions favorable to Pakistan.

The United States, with the rest of the world, is profoundly disturbed at Pakistan's handling of UN special representatives and truce teams. Continuation of this course of action is pointless and thoroughly damaging in every way.

Cable to U.S. Ambassador, Moscow: Convey our deep concern to the Soviet Government over the disappearance of the aircraft carrying Marshal Malinovsky and his delegation to New Delhi, expressing hope that the Marshal and his entourage may yet be found safe.

Cable to U.S. Ambassador, Bonn: Convey to the West German Government our disappointment at the Chancellor's views on U.S.-Soviet cooperation in the South Asian crisis. We believe it illogical to conclude, despite U.S. assurances and the continued presence of six U.S. divisions in West Germany, that our limited cooperation with the Soviets in bringing about a cessation of hostilities in South Asia represents the slightest threat to NATO or in any way affects West Germany's vital interests.

Cable to U.S. Ambassador, India: Inform the Indian Government that the United States is making every effort to secure Pakistan's withdrawal from disputed territory and her acceptance of UN arbitration. The United States will fully support the Indian position.

The United States will continue to support India in its conflict with Communist China. Aid will continue and, if necessary, be increased. It is our hope that the Indian Government will give careful thought to its support of Communist Chinese membership in the United Nations. A cessation of Sino-Indian hostilities purchased by such a concession will do little to stabilize long-term relations between the two countries.

The United States will, of course, lend every possible means of support to India in its attempts to restore internal stability. Requested aid will be provided promptly.

CONTROL NO. 18   GAME PAPER NO. 33
CONTROL TO ALL   MOVE PERIOD NO. (FINAL)

Scenario Projected from the Third Team Moves

In Ladakh, Chinese forces have halted their advance and are consolidating positions. The same applies to Sikkim, where no Chinese reinforcements are observed. In the NEFA area, Chinese forces continue to advance slowly and deliberately.

The Pakistani advance in Kashmir is similarly slow and deliberate.

The Soviet Union has readied an airborne division for dispatch to India to oppose Chinese aggression, if India considers this necessary. Afghanistan has granted overflight rights.

Nothing is changed so far as Indian and U.S. military matters are concerned. Strategic preparations in West Pakistan are proceeding. Elements of the 3rd Marine Division remain in Bangkok, being joined by other elements of same division. A U.S. carrier task force is cruising in the Bay of Bengal. No U.S. assistance has reached India beyond two squadrons of F-104s and limited riot control equipment. Other assistance is standing by.

The UN inspection team in Pakistan has finally surfaced and is being conducted to Kashmir. At the same time Pakistan has refused landing rights to the UN mission set down in Indian territory, claiming that this is a problem for India, not Pakistan.

The Soviet Union suspects, on the basis of no evidence, that the Soviet plane carrying Marshal Malinovsky and his delegation has been shot down by Communist Chinese fighters, although last reported over Soviet territory. It can now be revealed, with due deference to Soviet feelings, that the plane in question was not shot down but simply crashed into the side of a mountain. Communist China is justified in responding to any Soviet charges in this matter with manifestations of outraged dignity.

Re Kashmir and the Indian Border: China has offered to evacuate Sikkim in return for acceptance of a plebiscite solution of the Kashmir problem. The Pakistanis have not reacted favorably to the U.S. suggestion of UN arbitration of the Kashmir problem. The Pakistani position is that one Kashmir in the military hand is worth two in the arbitration bush. They continue to insist on a plebiscite, while toying with the idea of obtaining a U.S. guarantee that arbitration will achieve the same end. The Soviet position on the Kashmir problem appears to be more strongly adverse to Pakistan than that of the United States. The Soviets have suggested to the United States that under no circumstances should China and Pakistan be allowed to achieve their objectives "at gun point." They have simultaneously counseled the Indians to resist an arbitration solution, since this would be tantamount to surrendering Kashmir to Pakistan. The Soviet Union has indicated to the U.S. Government that it would prefer the formation of a UN force, incorporating Soviet and U.S. elements, for the relief of India, but failing Security Council action would understand unilateral U.S. military moves, particularly as the Indian Government would then doubtless request Soviet troops as well.

Re China's admission to the United Nations: Communist China has picked up U Thant's bait while continuing to refuse a "two Chinas" solution. Apparently feeling it has at least one foot in the UN door, however, China has invited U Thant to visit its glorious capital to discuss the matter further. Perhaps because of the Malinovsky incident, the Soviet Union has reconsidered its previously favorable attitude toward Communist China's admission to the United Nations; it has informed Peking that under present circumstances the Soviet Union cannot back Communist Chinese entry into the United Nations. Equally surprising is a U.S. reconsideration regarding Communist China's admission to the United Nations. President Johnson continues to reject giving her a seat in the UN Security Council, but suggests a U.S. willingness to let Communist China into the General Assembly, provided she withdraws from India and joins the nuclear test ban.

Otherwise there are these developments: Communist China makes obvious conciliatory moves toward the Soviet Union and the United States—in the latter instance seeking to head off a direct U.S. military involvement in India.

The United States is still trying to explain its position to the West German Government.

The Soviets seem intent on forging a *de facto* U.S.-Soviet alliance. They suggest that the United States pressure President de Gaulle to prevent any repetition of a French veto respecting United Nations military action in India.

The Warsaw Pact meeting apparently has broken up with inconclusive results. Apprehensions in Eastern Europe continue. At the same time the Soviets are apparently trying to exploit restiveness in Western Europe, particularly in West Germany, over U.S. Asian policy.

Prior to the concluding critique, the playing teams were given an opportunity to study the final scenario projection, together with game papers previously kept from their view. All participants were asked to offer projections of the situation beyond the concluding scenario. Were any lessons learned? And was there criticism of game technique or performance? In the reverse order of these three points, my summary of the critique follows.

Critique

The Yellow players complained Control had represented them as driving into the small neutral state of Sikkim beyond their intentions. Control properly countered this criticism by pointing out that the starting scenario provided for this development in advance; all Control had done was to keep things moving.

Blue asked, with some rancor, why the Yellow team had apparently ignored the presence of a U.S. carrier task force in the Bay of Bengal. Yellow wondered why Yellow should be particularly concerned, the Chinese forces being nestled within folds of the Himalayas. Was Blue threatening to drop nuclear bombs on the mountains? No, Blue was preparing

173

to attack Chinese forces should they debouch into the Assam plain of India. Well then, inasmuch as the Chinese troops stayed out of Assam, should they have panicked?

Blue was reproached for failing to establish clear enough objectives to meet the crisis, and for responding with words more than with deeds. Blue admitted that its initial approach to the problem was a "Band-Aid" approach, the object being to patch things up. The point was made that Blue might have missed an unprecedented opportunity to alter the entire political atmosphere, had it continued as timidly as its game efforts suggested it might, in view of the extraordinary changes shown in Soviet policy and attitudes.

Blue said that playing both the United States and India had appeared impossible as the game progressed, and that India had actually been left pretty much to Control. In future games, Blue thought, it would be inadvisable to put the affairs of two such countries in the hands of a single team.

The Yellow team, with agreement from both Blue and Control (but not from Red), considered that Red had overreacted, had shown too violent a bent, and had overdone the "togetherness" bit with respect to the United States.

The Game Director wondered if Communist China could really be pictured as wanting to join the United Nations as strongly as the progress of the game suggested. He also expressed surprise at the extent of the love affair that developed between the United States and the Soviet Union, although conceding that the starting scenario had been set up to produce a concert of U.S.-Soviet interest in opposition to that of Communist China.

All participants felt that the exercise had been highly educational. On the question of "lessons learned," however, the participants generally agreed that there were none of substance that should not have become evident from any serious

174

study of potentials present among the nations concerned. It was agreed that both the game and "serious study" could suggest three items of importance to the United States: solution of UN membership for Communist China, if any, would best be developed in something other than a crisis situation; any common U.S.-U.S.S.R. action outside Europe could have implications for relations between the United States and Western Europe; and the United States should be concerned at least as much with end objectives as with the means for dealing with *any* crisis.

An attempt was then made to project the game situation beyond the final scenario. It was agreed that the peace was definitely saved, for it would seem inconceivable that Communist China and Pakistan, or any combination of countries, could in 1966 militarily defy a coalition of the United States and the Soviet Union. Moreover, inasmuch as China was no longer pressing hard on India, massive assistance to India from either the United States or the Soviet Union would probably not be triggered.

It seemed apparent that, one way or another, Pakistan was likely to gain Kashmir, or a large part of it. The United States wound up committed in effect to such a solution, even though with Soviet opposition.

The chances of Communist China's eventual acceptance within the United Nations, if not entirely on her own terms, seemed to the gamers somewhat improved. For the first time, the United States had accepted in principle the idea of her admission.

All participants felt that the Sino-Soviet rift had become irreparable. Quite aside from the Malinovsky incident, the actions taken during the crisis by both—especially the Soviets —must prove to be lingering blows to "Socialist camp" unity. The implications of the rift for Soviet relations with Eastern Europe, while unpleasant for the Soviets, remain to be seen.

The Soviet Union has substantially strengthened its position in India. The Soviet Union, rather than the United States, strongly backed the Indian position and was also prepared to furnish substantial military support with no strings attached. If the Soviets made enemies of the Pakistani, they probably do not care.

U.S. difficulties in NATO have been measurably increased by the eagerness of the Soviet Union to cooperate with the United States in South Asia and by the affirmative nature of the U.S. response.

It was also felt that, although the immediate danger of serious warfare in South Asia has probably been averted and although some tenuous resolution of the Kashmir dispute appears in sight, the elements of conflict remain and have perhaps become more pronounced. Indians and Pakistani will hate each other no less. The Communist Chinese appetite for expansion has not been appeased. If anything, Peking's leverage on India may have been increased while Communist Chinese military prestige has hardly suffered. The United States, moreover, has demonstrated in the game no happy ability to discourage, with speed and precision, the kind of calculated and limited conquest which Communist China pursued during the fictional two weeks covered by the Kashmir crisis of 1966.

Chapter VIII

IS THE GAME WORTH A CANDLE?

Most participants develop an absorbing interest in the progress of a crisis game and are therefore likely to feel considerable enthusiasm for the technique. This enthusiasm develops, if for no other reason, because the game vehicle touches off an intense experience in group dynamics. For many players, no other payoff is nearly as important. Queried on the point, they may accordingly respond somewhat like the theatrical agent who was attempting to sell talent to the proprietor of a night club. "She's a beautiful blonde," he said, "with statistics of 58-22-35. Think of it! 58-22-35!" "Sounds good," said the night-club owner. "What can she do?" "What can she *do?* What can . . . well," replied the agent, "with a little help, she can sit up."

But in my own view, and that of others who have given consideration to crisis gaming, there can be no question that a well-conceived game is more than just a stimulating educational experience. Games produce other benefits as well, and sometimes very important ones. However, gaming has liabilities and limitations. Before dwelling on the plus side, we might examine some of the possible debits.

As a first item, the very vividness of the experience in communication, as Herman Kahn and Irving Mann point out, may dull the critical sense in players.[1] Patently, this is

[1] *Op. cit.,* p. 5.

bad, but it is not necessarily a *game* defect. A strong sense of participation may equally dull the critical sense in those responsible for handling real crises. If so, games may reflect at least this one characteristic of life. What appears at first sight to be a defect may actually be a merit.

The technique obviously holds no promise of prediction. Games do indeed turn up possibilities that later become realities. No means exists for determining *which* possibilities ought to carry the money, and in fact a chilling possibility in an official game can generate preventive action having the effect of making it less likely to occur, thus producing a sort of non-prediction. But if something can be done to de-fuse an unpleasant "contingent" possibility, turning up the possibility may offer as great a contribution to policy as a "categorical" prediction. Our Kashmir game, for example, suggested that Soviet-American togetherness in another part of the world could produce intense complications for U.S. relationships in Western Europe. Surely, if the two superpowers wished to concert their actions in Asia, or Africa for that matter, the United States would want to prepare the ground very carefully with its NATO allies.

If crisis gaming has the educational utility I accord it, it is a utility limited in practice to furthering the education of those who are already knowledgeable on political or military matters, or both. Undergraduates can of course learn something from any means of presenting material. A means without concrete rewards or penalties that, furthermore, asks a contribution of unscheduled time is evidently adapted only to dedicated students. Bernard C. Cohen reports, with respect to an exercise involving some ninety undergraduates at the University of Wisconsin,[2] that twenty to twenty-five were missing during each of two evening sessions. He cites this to indicate a high percentage of disinterest. In extenuation, however, the evening sessions took place during a warm May after what was presumably a hard northern winter. If males and females were distributed in anything like equal proportions, one might be entitled to wonder why any of them showed up. It was Lucian Pye's experience that undergraduate interest in political gaming was high when he experimented with the technique at M.I.T., but that considerable effort was required, especially of the professor.

As an important item in the litany of liabilities connected with crisis gaming, it is expensive in terms of the time of its participants. Responsible officials in Washington are harassed officials, who must ration their energies. Obviously they, unlike their academic counterparts, can hardly afford to invest much precious time in exercises having no certain payoff. Half a dozen Washington games in one year, generally employing different sets of participants, would probably approach an optimum number. There is no need to strain anywhere for a high number of games; the criteria might better be *interesting* rather than numerous situations.

Finally, on the debit side, if the play of a single game is time-consuming to an extent making economy in the selection of exercises advisable, it appears evident that the repetition of a single game, for the purpose of examining even a few variables, will in most cases be out of the question. But repetition of the kind achieved in computer games is impossible in any event. Use of a new set of players intro-

[2] "Political Gaming in the Classroom," *The Journal of Politics,* May 1962, p. 371.

duces an unmanageable number of variables resulting from differences in individual backgrounds and attitudes. And for the same set of players to repeat a game for the purpose of examining one or two alternatives is hardly more feasible, because, having lived through the exercise once, the players approach it another time at an enhanced level of sophistication and experience.

The "hand-played" crisis game provides, in fact, no more than an additional qualitative tool for the examination of essentially qualitative questions. Aspects of such questions that can be quantified or computerized are not the important ones. This is unfortunate, for analysis along nonquantitative lines is often less than satisfying in that it is not subject to clear proof. But it has to be accomplished, nevertheless, in connection with problems that are frequently of greater import in human affairs than those that can be solved beyond argument through statistics or the intersections of curves. The qualitative factor, therefore, often makes two minds better than one and many minds better than a few in addressing questions of international content. Here the individual act of creation almost never leads to settled policy or accomplished action except as it has been exposed to expert and often bruising scrutiny, the result of which in most cases burnishes the successful original concept to a higher degree of luster.

The Washington crisis game submits ideas to bruising scrutiny, certainly, but is it the scrutiny of those whose ideas count? A game played under academic auspices has the obvious value of providing a learning vehicle for people whose interest is in learning. The same exercise in Washington has less obvious value, because not many of the participants will be drawn from among the inner circle of decision makers likely to assist the President in handling an international crisis. We scarcely need the example of the

Cuban crisis in 1962, when President Kennedy admittedly relied for advice upon less than his entire Cabinet, to know that only a handful of Washington officials will live through a crisis with the Chief Executive. Pressure of time alone makes it evident that no President—or Prime Minister, or Chairman—can consult with more than a few officials when the chips are down. There are nevertheless good reasons why the numerous officials who advise *those* officials ought to engage in crisis gaming.

First, situations ought to be foreseen, and frequently handled in advance, at the same middle echelons of responsibility from which the majority of official gamers are likely to be drawn. This is the prime reason why crisis gaming can have a special value in Washington. The particular scenario utilized may have little specific application to oncoming realities, but it can suggest a type of problem that ought to be considered and it can arouse the less imaginative to keep antennae alert in attempting to head off international collision courses of any kind.

Beyond this, the official crisis game serves to introduce to one another, in a meaningful way, a good many officials who might otherwise meet for the first time only when handling *early* stages of a potential crisis situation which, if badly handled, could bring on an actual crisis at the highest levels of government. Confidence that might in such a circumstance be built painfully and with frequent misunderstandings can be fostered, among players in a game, at high speed and without risk of damage to the public interest.

The official Washington game, played for the most part at the level of middle policy makers, has another marked utility. Insights gained are not restricted to any official level. Rather, they have good prospects of permeating the entire structure of officialdom; down certainly, but also up. (Insights from unofficial games, because of the mobility possessed by ideas, are also quite capable of moving into governmental channels.) Crisis games stimulate and lubricate thinking, and thinking is the essential requirement in preparing to deal with international emergencies. Political planning, much less restricted in possibilities than military planning, can hardly develop contingency plans to meet more than a few obvious potentialities. The emphasis has to be on conceptual building blocks, ideas, and notions that can well become radiant and explicit as the result of a crisis game and the group dynamics it generates.

Recognizing its limitations, I therefore believe crisis gaming to hold distinct value both officially in Washington and at graduate academic levels. There is yet another important respect, moreover, in which it has scarcely been exploited. This is, to educate professional military officers in the *political* employment of military forces.

The obvious first professional task of military men is to be prepared to carry out their military assignments. If the military can't do this, whatever else they may do is hardly meaningful. But skilled and alert military forces will often be employed, in our thermonuclear era, through feints, maneuvers, and limited actions, to accomplish thoroughly limited political objectives. Professional military men have to understand this, and why it has to be, if they are to live with the inevitable frustrations imposed by politically restrictive limits. More than this, the interlocking of modern society and the new winds of global conflict have progressively eroded the traditional boundary markers between the battlegrounds and the pastures of politics—to the point where today's military professional, whether he is in the halls of the Pentagon or the rice paddies of Southeast Asia, is often called upon to make or participate in decisions which are truly more "political" than "military" in content and implication. To function effectively in the modern environment, therefore, he must have some feel for the analytical tools of diplomacy and international gamesmanship.

Crisis games conducted at military schools such as that of the Army at Leavenworth, Kansas, those of the Air Force at Maxwell Air Force Base, Alabama, of the Navy at Newport, Rhode Island, and of the Marines at Quantico, Virginia, as well as at the Armed Forces Staff College, Norfolk, Virginia, and at the various war colleges, could do much to achieve military understanding of limits that must be set politically on the uses of military force. Such games, assuming political advisers to participate with military officers, ought to provide heavy emphasis for a maxim of the ancient Chinese military sage, Sun Tzu: "The supreme art in war is to subdue the enemy without fighting." *Subdue*, like *pacify*, is an essentially political word.

There are, it should be added, a few respects in which one crisis game is likely to resemble another, and hence to suggest that validity can exist for the results.

Any kind of conflict game, for example, is virtually certain to produce unexpected difficulties of communication, and this is outstandingly true of political games. A degree of background noise exists for any communication process, as is well established in communication theory. Messages will fail to get through. They will be incompletely launched or garbled in transmission. They will be misunderstood in terms of semantics. In political situations, real or pretended, an additional problem exists because of the need for signaling intentions, suggesting warnings, and conveying nuances. Just how difficult this can be is likely to become evident in a crisis game, which nevertheless provides greater opportunities to explore the nature of this vital political communication problem than other means of studying politico-military processes. Schelling has been a perceptive student of this matter:

> . . . the misinterpretation that the sender of a message can perceive and anticipate, he can guard against; the ones that matter are those he cannot perceive in advance. The question then becomes, how do we identify the possible interpretations of a message that did not occur to the person who sent it? Putting it more crudely, and more generally, how can an analyst draw up a list of the things that would never occur to him? If the essence of the game is that there are two or more separate participants, two or more centers of consciousness and decision, we can generate understandings and misunderstandings.[3]

Bloomfield makes a similar point for the game technique as a whole when he says: "Inherent in [the politico-military gaming] process is the potent challenge of unpredictability and the equally potent value of exposure to the antagonistic will of another who proceeds from entirely different assumptions. Neither of these factors can be derived from solitary meditation or cooperative discussion."[4]

Schelling[5] again has emphasized a related point of

---

[3] T. C. Schelling, "Experimental Games and Bargaining Theory," *The International System; Theoretical Essays,* Klaus Knorr and Sidney Verba, eds., Princeton University Press, 1961, p. 49.

[4] "Three Experiments in Political Gaming," *The American Political Science Review,* March 1959, p. 1115.

[5] An apology would surely be in order for reliance on so few authorities, Bloomfield, Schelling, and Kahn among them, were it not that there *are* only a few authorities on the subject. It becomes difficult to recall which said it or did it first or best. A degree of confusion sets in, reminiscent of the couple who had suffered a particularly atrocious, resident mother-in-law problem during some twenty-five years. As they were preparing for a trip, finally, the husband said, "Dear, couldn't we just this once go away without taking your mother." His wife looked at him in astonishment. "*My* mother!" she said. "I thought she was *your* mother."

special interest in respect to the matter of communicating (in games, but also in life) with an international adversary. The playing teams display, with extraordinary consistency, the belief that they have communicated an unambiguously bold intent when in fact they have no more than settled on a bold program of action to meet future contingencies. In other words, having adopted a plan of action, which has been communicated to the Control team but otherwise held private, and having in most cases displayed to the opposing team no more than the first, generally timorous and tentative, moves emerging from the plan, a team is often satisfied that it has really told the opposition off! At least one lesson that may be expected to emerge from any crisis game is that signals, to be understood, have to be communicated loud and clear. Most game critiques can be depended upon to make this point, which in a sense comes through underscored as each group of antagonists, throughout the postmortem discussion, perseveres in the notion that it was they —*their* team—that came through the crisis triumphant, flag held high.

The game setting—any game setting—provides an especially encouraging atmosphere for the exploration of policy objectives, assumptions, preconceptions, and alternatives tied to a given scenario situation. People have little difficulty in agreeing on where to begin, because the problem has been thrown to them quite concretely and there is no alternative to getting on with it. In a conference, as Kahn and Mann point out,[6] after an initial period involving an exchange of views and an exploration of the issues, the tendency is "to stagnate into interminable arguments and dissensions or into feasts of argument" with very little con-

[6] *Op. cit.*, p. 8.

structive action. In a game, "the individual players take sides. They will study the problems associated with their sides with passionate interest and devotion. . . . There will be a real impetus to doing constructive work. . . ." Subsequently, the authors suggest—and the point is as valid for political gaming as for war gaming—that "the fact that the players themselves are pretending to take active roles in affairs forces them to think in a concrete and relatively responsible way about problems which they normally tend to discuss in lofty and abstract terms, often overlooking important qualifications."[7] Is it invidious to suspect that this observation may have a special aptness in scholarly circles?

As events evidently produce surprises even for a Chief Executive, a crisis game often produces surprises for the gamers, and this is one of its purposes. The exposition of preconceptions and assumptions is another, particularly useful in Washington, where officials are inclined at any given time to share the same preconceptions, and not invariably the correct ones. Outside participation, at least in the sense that the "outsiders" have not been as closely involved in the same problems and calculations as most of the participants, often has tonic effects in this connection. Again, for the official game, a frequently useful result is the provision of a real "feel" for the exercise of resources, in particular, military resources. Civilian officials achieve an enhanced appreciation of logistic and other problems associated with the movement of forces, after living through simulated days, weeks, or months of an unfolding deployment, and the insights gained may well have subsequent practical applications.

[7] *Op. cit.,* p. 9.

Certainly no one who has had to do with crisis gaming can believe that the technique, useful though it may be considered, offers a panacea for any purpose. On the other hand, I should be surprised to find any who feel that the uses of gaming have been fully plumbed, or that the technique is not subject to improvement. Putting "fact book" information on tape could alone offer an improvement. The experience of more people is bound to develop improvements. But applying the technique to a greater variety of problems is also a promising possibility.

The crisis game as I have described it is concerned essentially with international conflict involving superpowers. There is no apparent reason why the gaming of conflict has to be confined to that among international giants, or even to international conflict at all. On the latter point, it has already been suggested that forms of conflict other than international conflict might profitably be gamed. The domestic conflict of labor and management is an obvious such possibility. It presents no simple problem, for the interests concerned also include government and the public interest, which cynics might not regard as always identical. Experienced gamers could probably devise illuminating conflict situations, nevertheless, if aided and advised by experts in labor-management relations, by officials or ex-officials of the Department of Labor, and perhaps also by people who have served on arbitration panels. It should be a short jump to the time when specialists in labor-management matters could run such exercises without the help of outside "gaming" consultants.

Domestic political situations, from the national level on down, might also be explored in advance by application of game technique. Here, a solid representation of both the public interest and the public disinterest might shed a surprising degree of light on political issues, different in kind perhaps from the light shed by polling techniques.

The situation devised for the crisis in South Asia, covered in the previous chapter, was a complex one. The difficulty is that any situation designed these days to produce a plausible clash of the great world powers can hardly be simple. Uncomplicated confrontations, as in the past over Berlin, are hard to imagine.[8] Scenarios therefore have to involve smaller countries, playing active roles. An interesting approach, I should think, would be to attempt playing the small country roles as *principal* roles in a game, the superpowers being represented only on the Control team. American participants on contending teams in such an exercise would probably begin to feel a little like the officials of a small planet. Foreign participation might produce especially productive and interesting results, however, and there is no obvious reason to shy away from a mix of nationalities any more than from a mix of disciplines. Both could be good.

[8] As early as 1963 at the Hudson Institute, Herman Kahn was offering $500 for a scenario that *plausibly* brought on a general war between the United States and the Soviet Union. I believe this to have been a *bona fide* offer, although when I asked Mr. Kahn who would be the judge of plausibility, he said with massive dignity, "Me."

BIBLIOGRAPHY

Books

Duckworth, Eric, *A Guide to Operational Research*. London: Methuen & Co., Ltd., 1962.

Evans, G. W., III; Wallace, G. F.; Sutherland, G. L., *Simulation Using Digital Computers*. Englewood Cliffs, N.J.: Prentice-Hall, Inc., 1965.

Green, Bert F., Jr., *Digital Computers in Research*. New York: McGraw-Hill Book Co., 1963.

Guetzkow, Harold; Alger, Chadwick F.; Brody, Richard A.; Noel, Robert C.; Snyder, Richard C., *Simulation in International Relations: Developments for Research and Training*. Englewood Cliffs, N.J.: Prentice-Hall, Inc., 1963.

Kaplan, Morton A., *System and Process in International Politics*. New York: John Wiley & Sons, Inc., 1957.

McDonald, John, *Strategy in Poker, Business and War*. New York: W. W. Norton & Co., 1950.

Morschauer, Joseph, III, *How to Play War Games in Miniature*. New York: Walker & Co., 1962.

Schelling, Thomas C., *The Strategy of Conflict*. Cambridge, Mass.: Harvard University Press, 1960.

Periodicals

Abt, Clark C., "War Gaming," *International Science and Technology,* August 1964.

Bloomfield, Lincoln P., "Political Gaming," *U.S. Naval Institute Proceedings,* LXXXVI (September 1960), pp. 57–64.

Bloomfield, Lincoln P.; Padelford, Norman J., "Three Experiments in Political Gaming," *The American Political Science Review*, LIII (December 1959), pp. 1105–1115.

Cohen, Bernard C., "Political Gaming in the Classroom," *The Journal of Politics*, XXIV (May 1962), pp. 367–81.

Goldhamer, Herbert; Speier, Hans, "Some Observations on Political Gaming," *World Politics*, XII (October 1959), pp. 71–83.

Raymond, E. A.; Baer, Harry W., Jr., "A History of War Games," *The Reserve Officer*, XV, No. 10 (October 1938), pp. 19–20.

Rogers, Lindsay, "Notes on 'Political Science,'" *Political Science Quarterly*, LXXIX, No. 2 (June 1964), pp. 209–32.

Schelling, Thomas C., "War Without Pain, and Other Models," *World Politics*, XV, No. 3 (April 1963), pp. 465–87.

Ulam, Adam, "USA: Some Critical Reflections," *Survey*, No. 50 (January 1964).

Documents

Averch, H.; Lavin, M. M., *Simulation of Decision Making in Crises: Three Manual Gaming Experiments*, RAND Memorandum 4202-PR, August 1964.

Bloomfield, Lincoln P.; Whaley, Barton (of the Massachusetts Institute of Technology), *The Political-Military Exercise —a Progress Report*, unpublished draft article, August 16, 1963.

Cowper, William, *The Game of War*, Technical Operations, Inc., Burlington, Mass., 1960.

Davis, John B., Jr., *The Use of Gaming as an Aid in the Examination of National Security Problems of a Political Nature*, The National War College, Washington 25, D.C., 1964.

Hofman, Rudolf, General der Infanterie, *War Games*, Department of Army, Office of the Chief of Military History, MS P-094, Washington, D.C., 1952 (Draft translation).

Jenkins, James L., *Project OMEGA: A Collection of Simulation Models for the Study of Air War*, Technical Operations Inc., Washington, D.C., 1961.

BIBLIOGRAPHY

Kahn, Herman; Mann, Irwin, *War Gaming*, RAND Report P-1167, July 30, 1957.

McHugh, Francis J., *Fundamentals of War Gaming*, Naval War College, 1961.

Simulation and Gaming: A Symposium, AMA Report No. 55, American Management Association, Inc., New York, 1961.

Specht, Robert D., *War Games*, RAND Report P-1041, March 18, 1957.

Young, John P., *A Survey of Historical Developments in War Games*, ORO Report SP-98, March 1959.

G38